An Ethic of Excellence

*Building a Culture
of Craftsmanship
with Students*

Ron Berger

Heinemann
Portsmouth, NH

Heinemann

361 Hanover Street
Portsmouth, NH 03801–3912
www.heinemann.com

Offices and agents throughout the world

© 2003 by Ron Berger

Library of Congress Cataloging-in-Publication Data
Berger, Ron.
    An ethic of excellence : building a culture of craftsmanship with students / Ron Berger.
        p. cm.
    ISBN 0-325-00596-6 (pbk. : alk. paper)
    1. Teaching. 2. Academic achievement. 3. Excellence. I. Title.

LB1025.3.B467 2003
371.102—dc21

                                                        2003007290

Editor: Kate Montgomery
Acquiring editor: Lois Bridges
Production service: Colophon
Production coordinator: Lynne Reed
Cover design: Joni Doherty
Typesetter: Tom Allen, Pear Graphic Design
Manufacturing: Steve Bernier

Printed in the United States of America on acid-free paper
12   ML   14

Contents

Contents

Introduction

FOR TWENTY-FIVE YEARS I'VE LED A DOUBLE LIFE. I'M A FULL-time classroom teacher in a public school. In order to make ends meet for my family, I've worked during the summers, vacations, and sometimes weekends, as a carpenter. In the classroom or on the building site my passion is the same: If you're going to do something, I believe, you should do it well. You should sweat over it and make sure it's strong and accurate and beautiful and you should be proud of it.

In carpentry there is no higher compliment builders give to each other than this: That guy is a *craftsman*. This one word says it all. It connotes someone who has integrity and knowledge, who is dedicated to his work and who is proud of what he does and who he is. Someone who thinks carefully and does things well.

I want a classroom full of craftsmen. I want students whose work is strong and accurate and beautiful. Students who are proud of what they do, proud of how they respect both themselves and others.

When building a complex roof frame, some carpenters are adept at trigonometry and use calculators to figure rafter angles. Others never paid attention during high-school math and rely on a tape measure, spatial intelligence, and an experienced eye. In the end, as long as time and budget are reasonable, these differences don't matter. What matters is clear: a well-built house.

In my classroom I have students who come from homes full of books and students whose families own almost no books at all. I have students for whom reading, writing, and math come easily and students whose brains can't follow a line of text without reversing words and letters, students who can't line up numbers correctly on a page. I have students whose lives are generally easy and students with physical disabilities, and health or family problems that make life a struggle. I want them all to be craftsmen. Some may take a little longer to produce things, some many need to use extra strategies and resources. In the end, they need to be proud of their work and their work needs to be worthy of pride.

A few years ago I was crouched on the roof of a playhouse, nailing shingles with Aaron, one of my sixth-grade students. It was a glorious October Sunday, bright and crisp, one of those rare days that made me remember why I live in New England. The afternoon light was on the maple trees around us, the leaves yellow and scarlet, and from up there the world looked good.

Holly and Justine, fifth graders from my class, were painting trim down below and giggling about something. Mike showed up with his little sister and called up: I know I'm not in your class but could we help out, too? So they pitched in and soon Kate showed up and joined the crowd. With a crew of seven you might think we could finish the whole thing off quickly; it was only a playhouse. The truth was my class had been working almost every afternoon during school and after school for three weeks and still we had quite a way to go. Building with kids takes time.

I'll admit it was an elaborate playhouse. It was designed by my students in collaboration with their Kindergarten buddies as a service project during our study of architecture; it was a gift to the younger students of the school. By Kindergarten request, it was two stories tall with a stair-ladder inside, a "spy window" on the second floor, two windows on the first floor, and a front porch. It also had clapboard siding, Victorian trim details, and interior paneling. It wasn't that big, but it was nicely done.

I had argued repeatedly with my students that they were making a big mistake with their color choices: With pine green paint for the siding and cream colored trim, they had chosen green shingles. A green roof with green siding! I explained to them that it was going to clash and pleaded with them to consider a safer shingle color, something like black or tan. I got outvoted by my class. Turns out I was totally wrong. The shingles were a dark shade of gray-green that complemented the siding very well. My students received glowing comments from the community on their color choices. And don't think they didn't point this out to me all year long. As I was nailing off a shingle I noticed Aaron smiling at me. I know they look good, I said.

About ten years ago my double life actually became a triple life. In addition to teaching and building, I began working as a consultant for other schools. I felt the need to share my passion for excellence in education on a wider scale, particularly to work toward increasing educational opportunities for urban students. In the past few years my consulting work had been so busy that I had little time left for carpentry. It felt good to be pounding nails again.

Though my own school is in the back woods of Massachusetts, most of my consulting work is with city schools spread around the country. My students are mostly white, rural kids; the students and staffs I work with in cities are often non-white, sometimes with a variety of primary languages or cultures. My consulting work involves sharing strategies to help staff and students become motivated together about quality. To become excited about doing a good job.

I looked at Aaron carefully spacing roofing nails. I looked at the kids below me working together intently, installing clapboard and painting trim. I looked at this beautiful playhouse the students had designed and built. How do I share this?, I thought. How do I capture this?

The power of that Sunday was not really about New England

or playhouses. It was not about gifted kids, or clever teaching, or curriculum that should be marketed. There was a spirit, an *ethic* in the air that day. It was partly about the kids, the teaching, the curriculum, the school conditions, the community, but importantly, it was about all of these things at once. It transcended these things. It was the *culture* of the school that encouraged these kids to volunteer, to work together, and to care deeply about the quality of what they did. It was the ethic that this school culture instilled.

How do you share a culture? An ethic?

I'm concerned when I pick up a newspaper these days and so often find an article about the "crisis" in education and how a new quick fix will remedy things. More tests, teacher-proof curriculum, merit pay, state standards.

It reminds me of the advertisements for diet products. Fast Weight Loss! Dramatic Weight Loss! No Work! Lots of money is spent on diet products and a lot is spent on new educational tests. But it seems that almost everyone who loses weight quickly with the aid of a quick fix product ends up gaining it all back. Weighing yourself constantly doesn't make you lighter and testing children constantly doesn't make them smarter. The only way to really lose weight and keep it off, it seems, is to establish a new ethic—exercise more and eat more sensibly. It's not a quick fix. It's a long-term commitment. It's a way of life.

I have a hard time thinking about a quick *fix* for education because I don't think education is broken. Some schools are very good; some are not. Those that are good have an ethic, a culture, which supports and compels students to try and to succeed. Those schools that are not need a lot more than new tests and new mandates. They need to build a new culture and a new ethic. I don't believe there's a shortcut to building a new culture. It's a long-term commitment. It's a way of life.

I think as a nation we've gotten off track regarding education. Our concern seems to be centered on testing and ranking—ranking students, schools, and districts—over and over again. I believe our concern should be centered on what we can do in our schools and communities to bring out the best in kids.

In my work with schools across the country I sometimes encounter places where students are remarkably good at something. Working with my colleague Scott Gill, I learned that the high school his own children attend has a record in athletics that's hard to believe. This school, Cuba City High School in Cuba City, Wisconsin, is tiny: It has a graduating class of about seventy-five. The district is by no means wealthy; most families work in dairy farming or at the meat packing plant. In the past thirty years Cuba City has won fourteen state championships and forty-seven conference championships in a wide range of girl's and boy's sports. I have visited other schools that dominate state competitions in orchestra, chess, wrestling, visual arts, debate, and essay contests, and have done so for years, sometimes generations.

What's going on here? It doesn't seem likely that all the children born in Cuba City are good athletes, nor that all the great musicians live in one town in Iowa. I don't think this is genetics or luck. Private schools and universities can recruit talent, but these are public schools. Every year they take whatever kids they happen to get and make them stars. This phenomenon isn't limited to special areas, either. Cuba City, despite its demographics, has a stellar academic record. My colleagues at the Central Park East High School in Harlem and the Fenway High School in Boston work with urban students, almost all of whom are low-income and non-white, for whom the predicted graduation statistics are dismal. Both of these schools graduate 95 percent of their seniors and send about 90 percent on to college.

These schools don't have a gimmick, they don't have any special magic. We can say that they have high expectations for students, and this is certainly true. These schools have high expectations for students regardless of student background, race, or academic labels. Although almost every school in America claims to have "high expectations for every student," few schools actually do.

As a teacher, though, I can attest to the fact that high expectations guarantee nothing: they are simply the starting place. What is remarkable is that these schools make their high expectations manifest in student achievement, and they do this by sustaining school cultures that compel and support students to achieve. Newspaper articles on a successful urban school often choose one element of the school's culture and attribute the school's success to this single factor. It might be extended hours, school uniforms, tutors, or a classics curriculum. When I work with successful urban schools, it seems almost silly that anyone could imagine there is a single strategy—a magic bullet—that broke the cycle of failure in these poor communities. The challenges these schools face are broad and overwhelming and the school cultures they have built to address these challenges are complex and thoughtful.

The key to excellence is this: It is born from a culture. When children enter a family culture, a community culture, or a school culture that demands and supports excellence, they work to fit into that culture. A culture of excellence transcends race, class, and geography; it doesn't matter what color, income, or background the children come from. Once those children enter a culture with a powerful ethic, that ethic becomes their norm. It's what they know.

Two years ago I was asked to do a presentation on high-quality project work at The Austine School for the Deaf in Vermont. In addition to slides, videotapes, and samples of student work, I took along three of my sixth-grade students, Sonia, Lisa, and Chloe. All were hearing students but were, due to a class study of Deaf Culture, capable users of American Sign Language. In the morning we toured the school, visited classes, met students, and after lunch we did a presentation for the school staff. The students spread out their portfolios of work from the past two years and answered questions in sign language, with voice interpreting. The girls were thoughtful and articulate, and their work was stunning; I was very proud of them. So far things were going well.

When I concluded my presentation of slides and video, questions from the staff were directed to me and, equally, to the three students. The questions for the students centered primarily around one issue: what made them work so hard. Why do you have such high standards? Why do you prepare so many drafts? Why do you accept so much pressure? Why don't you complain or give up or turn in sloppy work?

The girls didn't quite get the questions. They were so much a part of the school culture, the town culture, that the questions didn't really make sense.

This is just the way school is, they finally said. It doesn't seem like high pressure—it's normal. This is the only school we know. Everybody does this many drafts, everybody worries about quality, everybody works hard. This is what school is about.

This book is an attempt to describe what an ethic of excellence can look like in a school, and to share strategies for building and sustaining a culture predicated on this ethic. The notion of excellence proposed here is broad—it includes academic and artistic excellence as well as excellence in character. It recognizes that schools play a major role in shaping values in children. Though society debates the question of whether schools should *teach values*, the process of schooling itself imbues values—we have no choice about this. If we want citizens who value integrity, respect, responsibility, compassion, and hard work, we need to build school cultures that model those attributes.

School cultures that support excellence can look very different from one another and can be housed in diverse settings; there is not one blueprint. The ideas in this book are garnered from a wide variety of educators whom I've had the privilege to read or to work with, from the work done by the staff of my school in trying to maintain such a culture, and from my own struggles to build a classroom culture of excellence.

This book is also the story of my quest to capture and share that culture in a way that can be useful to others, particularly to schools in need. To build a new culture, a new ethic, you need to begin somewhere. You need a focal point—a vision—to guide the direction for reform. The particular spark I try to share as a catalyst is a passion for beautiful student work and developing conditions that can make this work possible.

I use the phrase *beautiful work* broadly. Recently a teacher at the beginning of one of my presentations called out, My goodness! You've been talking so much about beautiful work that I thought you were an art teacher; this stuff is math and science. As a fifth and sixth grade teacher in a small town I teach all subjects; work of excellence in any discipline is beautiful to me and I don't hesitate to label it so.

I believe that work of excellence is transformational. Once a student sees that he or she is capable of excellence, that student is never quite the same. There is a new self-image, a new notion of possibility. There is an appetite for excellence. After students have had a taste of excellence, they're never quite satisfied with less; they're always hungry. When the teachers at the Austine School for the Deaf pointed out to Sonia that many students wouldn't obsess over their work as she does, her reply was quick: This school has ruined me for life, she said. I'm never satisfied with anything until it's almost perfect. I have to be proud of it.

At its core, my consulting with schools and districts is an effort to share the power and the pride of this ethic of craftsmanship. Most students, I believe, are caught on school treadmills that focus on *quantity* of work rather than *quality* of work. Students crank out endless final products every day and night. Teachers *correct* volumes of such low-quality work; it's returned to the students and often tossed in the wastebasket. Little in it is memorable or significant, and little in it engenders personal or community pride. I feel that schools need to get off this treadmill approach and shift their focus from quantity to quality.

My builder friends make fun of architects. I have great respect for architects; I have a few as friends and am indebted to the many architects who have come to my classroom to share their knowledge and to critique student design work. I have to confess though: I join right in during the architect-bashing lunch breaks at the construction site. The argument is always the same. Architects would never design all these screwy things if they actually had to build them. When you're a builder you know what makes sense and it seems that architects don't seem to have a clue about this. They don't have any real, practical knowledge, just fancy ideas.

Architects have identical, if opposite, dialogues—builder-bashing discussions: You can't trust builders to follow the plans. Builders always make changes and cut corners, always think they know better. They just want to stick with what they're used to and hate creative new ideas or innovations in design.

Who's right here? Both sides are important. Both need to be listened to and taken seriously. In the end, both voices are treated with respect by anyone putting up a building.

I wish I could say the same for the national dialogue on education. We've got a lot of designers with ideas for improving schools, but no one seems to be talking to the builders. The architects of educational policy get a lot of attention in the media, but there is a voice that seems left out of this dialogue—the teachers. My motivation for writing this book is to introduce another rare teacher voice into this discourse.

I can't speak for others. All I can offer is a single, personal perspective. I can promise though that it is a voice from the building site, not from the architecture firm. Even though a goal of excellence in education is one we all share, the notion of how to get there may sound very different in these pages than it sounds in campaign speeches or newspaper headlines. As every teacher knows, you can mandate tests and standards and curricula all you want, but it means nothing if you can't inspire kids to care.

In my work as a carpenter, the first thing I do when I arrive at a job site is unload my toolboxes. In my work as an educational consultant, the first thing I do when I arrive at a school site is the same: I unload my education toolboxes, metaphorically speaking.

I bring no blueprint for school change. As I mentioned, I believe each school is different and there are many models of excellence. But I have tools to share, ones that I've borrowed from others, and ones that I've built myself. My hope is that at least some of those tools will prove useful to others. The tools I offer here are *strategies*, *models*, and *metaphors*, and along with them I have classroom stories that I hope put these tools in context and make them clear and human.

I have three toolboxes; each has a dedicated chapter in this book.

The first toolbox, Chapter Two, is concerned with building a foundation for *A School Culture of Excellence*. Particular strategies for improving student work and thinking are almost useless unless they're embedded in a community that encourages and supports excellence.

The second toolbox, Chapter Three, is a big, heavy one. It contains strategies for building *Work of Excellence*. This box is the heart of my work with schools, and describes practical suggestions for improving the quality of student work and thinking.

The last toolbox, Chapter Four, concerns the *Teaching of*

Excellence. Much of the country seems seduced at the moment with visions of *teacher-proof* curriculum, where teachers are seen as little more than semi-skilled gas station attendants *delivering curriculum* into student brains. I'm not sure what these people are thinking. Anyone who has spent time in a school classroom remembers well the difference between weak teaching and inspirational teaching.

Of course in real life these metaphoric toolboxes are not actually discrete, nor are the tools inside; the boxes and tools are all interrelated. I have chosen to describe them as discrete here in an effort to make the strategies more easily referenced by the reader. My hope in sharing this perspective on schooling and in sharing these strategies is the same here as when I work with schools personally: that something in this approach or collection of tools, even a small thing, may prove useful.

Before unpacking these toolboxes for the reader, I have included an opening chapter to give the reader a sense of my vision of craftsmanship and excellence. Chapter One tells the story of my quest to share this vision with educators.

CHAPTER ONE

An Archiver of Excellence

Evidence in the Work

IT'S A SNOWY FRIDAY NIGHT, 11:30 P.M. THE PITTSBURGH airport is deserted. I'm standing at a silver baggage claim carousel, praying. No more bags are coming down the chute, no more passengers are waiting at the edge. The same lonely unclaimed suitcases are making the rounds again. At least they're still moving. At least there's still hope. Then the machine shuts down and there's a terrible, final silence. I stand alone and shake my head.

They can't have lost my bags. It's not possible. At 9:00 in the morning I'm giving the keynote speech at an education conference. Everything I need is in those bags. I stare at the carousel in disbelief, waiting for the noise to resume. This can't be happening to me.

I'm not famous. No one at the conference will have a clue who I am. I'm just a teacher, a public elementary school teacher in a tiny town no one has heard of, not even people in my own state. But I have something special, and that's why they invited me. I have a big black portfolio of unforgettable student work. I have 140 slides of stunning student projects. I have videotapes of students presenting their work that seem too good to be true. I have all of these things—now lost somewhere in the airports of America!

They can't have lost my student work. This work is more precious than anything I own. It's irreplaceable. My students will kill me. My former students will kill me. I'll have no models for my future students. And, at the moment, have nothing, nothing as evidence for tomorrow's audience. I stare down at my old jeans and work boots. If I had to, I could present in these clothes. I would look silly, but no one would be looking much at me once the slides began. But without the work! I might as well fly back home. This is a nightmare.

We're awfully sorry for the inconvenience, sir, a woman at the baggage claims office informs me. But don't worry . . . we find almost all bags, and we find almost 90 percent of them within twenty-four hours. She hands me a little plastic bag containing a tiny gray toothbrush and a tube holding one serving of toothpaste. Would you like a disposable razor, too? I'm speechless. I stare at her, look at the toothbrush, and I can't think of what to say. This can't be happening. In a daze, I stagger out into the snowy night with my toothbrush and stumble onto a shuttle bus. No bags, sir? asks the driver.

I can't sleep. I sit up all night at a cramped hotel room desk with my carry-on backpack, reading through student papers turned in that day. I feel nervous and ill.

It had been a lousy Friday at school—my students had been distracted, some of them ill behaved; I'd been impatient and frustrated. As I read through their work with bleary eyes it all looks awful. How could they write like this at this point in the year? What kind of teacher am I? Not only did I have nothing to show tomorrow but I was an imposter too: a failure as a teacher.

Then about 3:00 A.M. I read through a descriptive piece by a fifth-grade girl and I stop. I read it over and over. How could she have written this herself? It's so powerful, so evocative, so sophisticated. She must have gotten help. But she couldn't have—I watched her write it in class yesterday. It is really her work.

She's a girl with some learning disabilities but with wonderfully expressive language skills. She's not confident or articulate verbally, but on paper she's another person. Her prose is so lyric it often reads like poetry. Even knowing her skill, this piece is arresting—it just sings. I stare at it, fully understanding what a gift I've just received. I will photocopy this piece as a model, not just for my current students but also for students in years to come. This is a piece of writing for setting standards. It lifts me, for a moment, from my nightmare.

I put aside the work and crawl onto the bed and shut the light. Fully clothed, on top of the hotel bedspread, I fall into troubled sleep.

About 5:30 A.M. I'm startled from sleep by a loud knock on the door. I stagger in the dark panicked and confused about where I am, and open the door to find a cheerful young man in a uniform with my baggage. I'm so stunned that he's gone before I realize I should have given him a tip. A gigantic tip. Everything in my wallet would have seemed too small.

While shaving I notice how red my eyes are. Since injuring my corneas in a carpentry accident, my eyes are easily irritated and inflamed; dust, smoke, or dryness leaves them ragged. A night with no sleep gives me the eyes of a derelict. Eye drops do nothing to help them. Usually I am self-conscious to meet anyone looking like this but this morning I realize it doesn't even matter. Nothing matters: I've got the work. I've got the work. I smile a tired smile at the mirror.

At the conference I am greeted by a slim, gray-haired woman in a dark business suit, a superintendent. I read her nametag but don't recognize the name as someone with whom I've corresponded about the conference. She introduces herself and hands me a nametag that says "Dr. Berger." I'm a bit embarrassed and explain that I'm not a doctor, just a teacher. She's flustered and says there's no time to make a new tag. You're not with a university? She's in disbelief. No Ph.D.? I'm supposed to introduce you, she says. What do I say about you? When I explain that I teach elementary school and work as a builder she grows even more flustered; she walks away and returns. She asks me if I would mind introducing myself. Fine, I say. And it is fine. Even though she is rude and condescending it doesn't matter, because I've got the work now and everything will be fine.

I walk up on stage and look out over a wide sea of faces and introduce myself: a public school teacher from Massachusetts. The faces are tired and skeptical—those of teachers and administrators dragged away from home on a Saturday morning, wishing they were home having breakfast with their families. This conference is not really a conference. The audience didn't sign up to come here, excited to learn new things. It's a multi-district inservice day: a workshop that is mandatory for school staff to attend, or so strongly encouraged that it might as well be mandatory. In either case, it's not an audience of smiles.

After just a few minutes of speaking I can see the eyes in the front row glaze over. No one is snoring yet but it's just a matter of time. But then I kill the lights and begin the slides—and the magic begins. People start to sit up, whispering to each other as I speak. They point to things on the screen and interrupt with questions. There's some electricity in the room. The work is too powerful to ignore.

I show slides of a field guide to local amphibians created by a third grader in my colleague Ken Lindsay's class. People gasp. It's impossibly beautiful. Did you say *third grade*, someone shouts out. *Third grade*? Is this a school for the gifted? I show slides of original amphibian research done by Ken's third and fourth graders—collection, mapping, reporting data to the state. I show slides of the world's first salamander tunnels built under a road to protect migrating salamanders, with state-fabricated *Salamander Crossing* road signs designed by one of Ken's students.

I show slides of my sixth-grade students managing a scientific project, done in collaboration with a local college laboratory, done to test the town's homes for radon gas. The slides show students preparing surveys, kits, and informational packets for the families in town, learning the Microsoft Excel spreadsheet program to do data analysis of results; and show pages from their final radon report for the town. The report turned out to be the first comprehensive radon picture of any town in the state. It was not only used by our town: After being featured in the media, the report was requested by towns all over the state, by the state radon commission, and by the federal radon commission. The slides show a classroom transformed into something like a non-profit company, printing copies of the report, responding to requests and questions with individual cover letters, and mailing off copies. All of this run by students. They did the analysis, wrote the report, responded to inquiries, and when the phone rang—whether it was a concerned family, the town lawyer, the media, or real estate agents—it was students who went down to the office to do the talking.

How can kids be trusted with such important work?, someone asks. Let me tell you, I say. Sometimes I need to be a tyrant for accuracy and quality in my classroom. Not this time. The students were scared to death. Scared that any possible error in their math would jeopardize the safety of a real family in town. Scared that their page in the report might have a grammatical or statistical error. Scared that the school would be in legal trouble if real estate values changed or if families moved based on mistakes in their data. These students checked their math, their spelling, their language, and their reasoning twenty times over before they rested easy. They begged me to check their work over again. This was not an exercise: It was real, important work that mattered to the world. Anything short of excellence would be intolerable.

I show slides of projects by individual students of different ages, Kindergarten through sixth grade. The work is done by students in all classrooms in my school and it's beautiful and powerful; I feel proud to have the chance to show it, proud to work in a school with colleagues who elicit such work.

While showing one slide I'm interrupted. Wait a minute here, a gentleman in the front says. That does not look like the work of a child. The slide is a blueprint of a house drafted to scale, seen in plan view—bird's eye view. The scale is standard architectural scale, one quarter inch equals one foot, and has been drawn with standard professional tools—drafting pencils, erasers and ink, architectural scale rulers, templates and squares. The lettering is hand-done architectural printing, precise and consistent. The blueprint includes furniture and is colored with professional-quality colored pencils; the carpeting, tiles, countertops, flooring, and furniture fabrics are all original choices and designs done by the student. This particular home has southwestern style rugs, ceramic tiles in the kitchen, baths, a greenhouse, and furniture designed with Navaho patterns. There's a fountain in the greenhouse shaded exquisitely with blues, aquas, and white foam colors.

I'm in luck here, I tell the gentleman. I happen to have this very blueprint here with me today—the original—in my portfolio, along with five or six earlier drafts of the work. I invite him to come look at it after the presentation and get a sense of the process involved in creating it.

A large portion of the audience is comprised of African American educators. In many ways this is a blessing. When I share my stories, my struggles, my joys in student successes, they don't sit quietly like some audiences do. This audience calls out affirmations when they agree or sympathize, and when they disagree they let me know. The auditorium is filled with spirit and life.

It's also a challenge. I know the first thing my audience sees is that I'm white. I'm a white man in a suit who works mostly with white children. There's no way in the world, they're thinking, that I could understand their situations. I need to find our common ground and make it obvious. We do have common ground; we do have a bond. The people in this audience dedicate their lives to the same thing that I do; they have the same frustrations and self-doubts, the same joys and victories. I work to build this connection. I don't want all this precious student work discounted because of my background and setting.

Where are the black faces?, someone calls out. These are all rich white kids!

They're mostly white, yes, I say. But they're not rich. I show slides of my town. There is not a single store in town, not a single traffic light. More than two-thirds of the town roads are dirt, including the road I live on, and there is a good portion of the year when I need to have my truck in four-wheel drive just to get to school in the morning. The town made the local paper recently with a photograph of a federal census taker going from house to house on horseback because the mud was so bad her car was useless.

Other than homes, the town has essentially seven buildings: an old white New England church, the post office (a little white house), the town hall (the old two-room schoolhouse), a tiny library, the volunteer fire shed, a bar, and the school. That's it. There are lots of beautiful trees and streams, even a lake, but this isn't Beverly Hills.

I know your world, shouts a large woman from the back. Ya'll are *country*! We know *country*, she says, and she laughs. The audience smiles and nods.

It's good we have a connection, because now I show slides of my classroom and it makes my differences all the more plain.

That's a *classroom*? A woman points at the slide and turns to her row of friends. No way that's a *classroom*.

My classroom has no desks. There are folding tables where students sit for lessons and work, but in this slide the tables are folded against the wall and students sit in a circle on the rug for a group meeting. The classroom is filled with furniture I designed and built with local wood, there are shelves for books and student sculptures and models, a student-built light table for drafting work, colorful student work displayed on almost every bit of wall space, hanging plants, large quartz crystal clusters and fossils on display, sculptures of turtles, a couch for reading, and near the center of the room a bathtub which has been framed in a wooden box containing rocks, plants, a waterfall, and live local turtles swimming in the current.

The woman shakes her head. That's a *science museum* or a *library*. That's no classroom. You said this is *public* school?

I explain that since we are a small school in a one-school district, the staff has been able to make decisions as a group. We've allowed teachers to design their classrooms. Some have student desks and some, like mine, use tables instead. The fact that things are arranged artistically and kept so clean and neat is my own need: I'm a bit obsessive, I admit to them. My students work hard to keep the room tidy and beautiful. I show slides of my colleague Ken's third- and fourth-grade room that looks even less like a classroom: Every possible space is covered with glass aquariums full of pond life, white buckets of pond water are on the floor, on the wall is a gigantic map of the town marked with vernal ponds and wetlands, and students are carrying nets and jars as they walk around.

We're a different-looking school but, yes, we're a regular public school, the only school in town.

An elegant young African American woman introduces herself as a school principal and compliments the work and ideas. This work is beautiful, she says. And shows real skills. Then she asks an important question. But how do we know this doesn't just represent the work of your best, your brightest students. Unless we visit your school, we can't know what's truly representative of what goes on there.

A fair question and a perceptive one. You can't know for sure, I say, and you have no real reason to trust me. Come visit my school. We would welcome you, and my students would be delighted to share with you the portfolios of their work. Until then, I have some slides that may help with this understanding.

I have put together a short series of slides that are perhaps the most valuable evidence I have to share. The slides tell the story of single piece of work through many stages and drafts, and tell the story of the child who struggled with its creation. This sixth-grade girl and her mother graciously allowed me to photograph not just the work but also their lives, and allowed me to speak honestly about all of it.

I begin with a slide of a cross-sectional blueprint of a cave home. It's an impressive piece of work, similar in quality to the work in all the slides I had been showing this morning. Then I explain that while the blueprint may look like the work of an academically gifted child, it was done by a student with substantial special needs. The following slides give a little background on this student.

Jenny, as seen in the slides, is a smiling girl with long brown hair wearing an old gray sweatshirt. Various photos show her sitting on the gate of a rusty old pick-up truck, standing by a small corral in the woods feeding her horse, squatting by her rabbit hutch. Jenny cares for her animals herself buying feed with her babysitting money and she is one of the most sought-after babysitters in town. In the realm of real life, she is a star: confident, creative, hardworking, responsible, polite. As a babysitter she is as reliable and talented as they come.

In the realm of school, Jenny struggles. Her learning disabilities mean that reading, writing, and math come to her with tremendous work, and sometimes a lot of tears. But Jenny's indomitable spirit makes her a pleasure to have as a student. I show a slide of Jenny as a first grader standing next to her first published book which is on display in the school library. The book may have been very difficult to create but she's standing tall and proud.

Then I share a slide of Jenny's first draft of this sixth-grade project. There is quiet in the audience. The work is messy and primitive. It shows conceptual and spatial confusion: It's hard to even understand what the drawing represents. I explain that Jenny was so ashamed of this draft that she told me, with tears in her eyes, that she didn't want it posted on the board for the class critique session. This was fine, I said, and I asked her to get private critique from her friend Nicole.

The next slide shows the second draft, prepared after receiving suggestions and support from Nicole. This draft is much clearer and better planned, and shows some understanding of the concept of cross-section. Jenny felt much more confident about this draft and agreed to have it pinned up for class critique. The feedback she received from the group is incorporated into draft three, shown on the next slide. The critical feedback that Jenny received from her fellow students indicated that they preferred her second draft to her third and she was upset; how could this draft not be better—it was her latest draft? But a new draft is not always a better draft, and Jenny returned to the drawing board to work on an improved draft four.

Jenny took the strongest parts of draft two and three and combined them in the fourth draft. This draft looks strong. The layout is clear and sensible; there is careful artistic shading on the rocks, the rooms are correctly labeled. At this point in the creation process, Jenny said to me, Mr. B, I hate my messy writing on this project and I know you teach calligraphy so could you teach it to me . . . really fast? I told Jenny that I couldn't teach it to her "really fast" but I gave her some sheets of calligraphy and had her practice by tracing it on the class light table. After four days of tracing, her writing showed amazing growth, which is shown on a slide of her post-practice freehand calligraphy.

I show a slide of draft five, the final draft, and not only is the drafting work excellent but the lettering is neat and calligraphic. It's a beautiful piece of work. Suddenly the audience realizes that this is basically the same slide they had viewed earlier, except it looks different now. Five minutes ago they saw just another project by an anonymous, talented kid. Now the struggle, work, and growth that this project represented was evident. Now it's clear that the quality of work I had been showing the audience all morning is not the result of gifted students nor specially selected students: It is a celebration of hard work, dedication, support, critique, and revision. It is the fruit of sweat and care. It showcases more than anything a school ethic and culture that compels students to achieve more than they think possible.

One advantage to living and teaching in a small town is that I know where most of my former students have gone with their lives. I am happy to be able to say that this particular student, Jenny, never lost her spirit. As with most academically challenged students, her learning disabilities didn't magically disappear as she grew older. But Jenny continued to get support and continued to succeed. In eighth grade Jenny won a graphic contest sponsored by a local newspaper; when she called me up, it brought tears to my eyes. In ninth grade Jenny took a day off from high school to return to my classroom to help a student with cerebral palsy on a cave exploring trip. Unlike many students in America with similar backgrounds, Jenny got her high school diploma and then went on to college, entering the University of Massachusetts Stockbridge School of Agriculture. Last May I attended her college graduation party and I can't remember being more proud of any student.

The talk ends in Pittsburgh and I'm surrounded by teachers and administrators who want to share ideas. We're on common ground and it feels good. The superintendent who declined to introduce me is nowhere to be seen. There are compliments from all sides, which I promise to convey to my students—it is they who deserve them, I say. And they do.

As I board the plane to fly home I think of the deliveryman who brought my bags and I smile. If only I'd been awake enough to tip him.

Evidence in the Students

Sometimes even having models of student work is not quite enough. I got a call one summer evening from Dennie Wolf, a colleague and mentor who ran a research group called Performance Assessment Collaborative for Education (PACE). Dennie is an expert in assessment and she helped my school refine its use of portfolios; we were fortunate to be part of the PACE network of schools. Now Dennie needed a small favor. Some of the foundations that funded PACE were reviewing their grants and wanted to see evidence of student progress. She asked if I could bring some student work to share at a meeting.

I was in the middle of building a house addition but I checked with my partner and he didn't mind if I took a day off. I told Dennie sure. The next morning I moved the tools and sawhorses out of my truck, filled it with portfolios and slides of student work, and drove across the state to Cambridge, Massachusetts. I thought this would be a typical presentation: skeptical people with little interest in what I have to share until they saw the work. Then, the change—real interest and great dialogue, discussion about the work and the steps needed to create it.

I was wrong. This day was hard from start to finish.

I left the truck in an expensive parking garage and stumbled through crowded streets with boxes and bags of student projects. On the Harvard campus I was directed to a fancy conference room where an elegant luncheon was set out and a roomful of very well-dressed men and women sat talking. I was seated at a table set with more forks than I knew what to do with, and my boxes and bags of work were discretely taken away to the corner of the room where they wouldn't clutter the space. I looked down at my hands. They were scrubbed clean but were scored with cuts from metal flashing and stained with roofing tar. I should have used more paint thinner on my fingers. There was no place on this luncheon table to spread out novels, scientific reports, mathematical graphs, blueprints, posters, and models. My portfolios, boxes, and slides were in the corner and it was clear that's where they would stay. What in the heck was I doing here?

I sat quietly throughout the luncheon, keeping my hands on my lap whenever possible. Then the discussion suddenly turned my way. Hugh Price, then at the Rockefeller Foundation, now the head of the National Urban League, had been speaking eloquently about standards in education. I noticed he used a number of sports metaphors and guessed that he had probably been a successful scholastic athlete himself. After speaking about high jumping and raising the bar for schools he turned and addressed me: Dennie tells me your school has been using portfolio assessment for over fifteen years. Tell me, how are your test scores now versus fifteen years ago?

I looked painfully over at my portfolios leaning against the fancy wallpaper and looked back to the table. Where should I go with this? Well, Mr. Price, my school performs well on standardized tests. But I was hoping I could share a different type of evidence with you.

If we're trying to see if portfolio assessment can help schools raise the bar, he replied, we need a tangible measure of success. It's just like in high jumping: A test shows how high you can jump. This is what we need to know.

I hesitated before I spoke. I wanted to say: That's the wrong metaphor. Everyone talks about raising the bar as if the broad range of attributes we hope to develop in students—character, work ethic, attitudes, academic skills, understanding, thinking strategies, social ethics, and skills—could be measured by jumping over a single bar. This is crazy. But I didn't say this.

Mr. Price, I know you want tangible evidence. All people do: parents, community members, and policy makers. But I think we've come to believe that there is only one type of evidence—numerical scores—and I think there are other types of evidence that are just as important. *More* important. I was hoping I could show you this.

There was no hope of clearing off the plates and glasses to make room for student work, but Dennie saved me here. She had a VCR rolled into the room. If I couldn't share the work, at least I could show a short videotape of a student doing so. I asked for the group's patience in watching a ten-minute presentation.

A sixth-grade girl appeared on the video, a small girl with a cast on her broken hand and a quiet smile. This student, Jamie, was presenting herself and her work to a panel of educators in a mandatory graduation requirement: final portfolio presentations. The panel consisted of teachers from the junior high school she would attend in the fall, members of the community and the school committee, and educators from other schools. Graduation by exhibition—the idea of requiring students to maintain portfolios of their work in all disciplines and to formally present their competence and skills to a panel in order to graduate—was not something we invented. A number of schools had pioneered this notion, most notably Deborah Meier's Central Park East schools in Harlem and other members of Ted Sizer's Coalition of Essential Schools.

Jamie spoke while her friend and assistant Melanie handed work to the panel and posted work on display boards. What was captivating about the presentation was not that Jamie was a star in all academic areas. Like most students, she had her strong areas and her weak ones. Though an inspired worker, Jamie had learning challenges in written language and was candid and articulate in describing these. The power of Jamie's presentation was in her incredible poise and pride in describing her work and in her incisive understanding of her strengths, difficulties, and goals. She took her learning seriously and her work ethic, as evidenced by her passion and her many drafts of papers and projects, was inspirational. Jamie shared beautiful final drafts of her work but also described the struggles and mistakes that were embodied in earlier drafts. She shared architectural blueprints, a children's science book, a fictional character study, mathematical finance work, business letters, artwork, and more. She fielded questions from the panel with grace and humor.

After ten minutes we shut off the VCR and there was silence. Hugh Price turned back to the table with a big smile. You are right, he said with a chuckle, this is powerful evidence. If every school-child in America could present herself like this we'd have nothing to worry about in American education. That was inspiring.

A number of people around the table agreed that after that pres-entation they would have hired Jamie for a position in their firm in a minute, or offered her a spot in an elite private school just as eas-ily. A gentleman remarked that if his own son, a high school student at a prestigious school, could present himself with half of Jamie's composure and insight he'd be overjoyed.

But not all were convinced of the value of this evidence. Anyone can pick an exemplary student, they said. We can't rate a school based on one student. Others remarked that this was again a privileged white school, not a challenged urban school. One gentle-man said the whole thing could easily be rehearsed and staged and he didn't trust it at all.

I considered the merit of trying to convince the panel that this wasn't a privileged school, nor was Jamie the *star* student. But if that videotape didn't move them, my words would be useless. I had a dif-ferent idea. The group was meeting for two days. I spoke with Dennie and she asked the group if they would be interested in meeting a number of students the following day, students with portfolios of their work, and have the opportunity to question the students in person. To examine the evidence first hand. The sched-ule for tomorrow was busy, but it was agreed that during the lunch break we could set up a display of student work in an adjoining room, with students representing their portfolios. Panel members could visit if they wished.

I had some scrambling to do. I drove home and called my build-ing partner and told him I'd be out an extra day. I phoned around to find students who were free to go with me to Cambridge the next day, and managed to line up four, including Jamie. Missing one day of summer vacation to present their work at Harvard didn't sound so bad. I rounded up their portfolios from their homes and loaded them in my truck, and the town minister agreed to drive the students the following morning. (My truck could never fit them.)

The kids arrived at Harvard wearing their Sunday best. Their clothing alone said a lot—these were not rich kids in casual designer clothes; they were country kids dressed to visit the city, wanting to look their best and be polite. They walked in with panic on their faces. I was surprised. They'd presented their work many times before—to families, school guests, the graduation panel. What was different here?

Where are our portfolios!? They looked around frantically. I showed them the presentation room with their work on the tables and they breathed a sigh of relief. They scurried around setting up displays of their work and then paused and looked up with confident smiles. I understood. They were panicked because they didn't have the work. I'd been in that situation myself, I recalled. Now they had the work in hand, and everything was just fine.

I'll share just one story from that wonderful lunchtime presentation scene. Partway through the lunchtime exhibition the most skeptical of the panelists, the one who felt that the whole thing could easily be rehearsed and staged, entered the room. He recognized Jamie from her video and walked over to her table.

Ahh, he said. I recognize you from your presentation; we saw you on videotape yesterday. You're Jamie. Tell me something, Jamie. You spoke quite well on that video. Are you a good writer?

Jamie paused and looked down. That's a difficult question, she said. Do you have a little time?

The gentleman smiled.

Being a good writer means a lot of different things, she said. I'm not sure where I should begin. My expressive writing is pretty strong, as is my fiction and even my essays. I have good story ideas and I can clearly express opinions in my work. Let me show you some examples . . . here is my character file project, these are drafts, these are finals; here are some of my essays in final draft. I also work very hard at my writing, which you might be able to tell from the number of drafts here and the kinds of revisions.

But I have some serious weaknesses in writing, too. I'm dyslexic and I just can't spell. I need to use all kinds of strategies for my spelling. You can see this in the early drafts of these business letters. My problems with spelling had an effect on my punctuation habits, too. Maybe I could take you through a number of drafts of one piece of work and you can see some of my strengths and weaknesses . . .

The gentleman asked to be excused for a moment and returned with a chair. He sat down next to Jamie and together they began to read through her work, looking at where she'd been as a writer and where she needed to go next. I left to listen in on other presentations and when I returned, quite a while later, the two of them were still engaged in discussion, smiling and pointing to the work.

I was no longer worried about arguing the value of portfolios to this panel. The funding for PACE continued and I was proud that my students could be of help.

A few years later I got a letter from Jamie with an essay that she'd written in high school enclosed. Asked to write about an event that had changed her life, she chose to write about the time she was asked to go to Harvard University to present her work.

A Library of Excellence

One of my jobs as a teacher, I feel, is to be an historian of excellence, an archiver of excellence. Wherever I am, in my school or in other schools throughout the country, I am on the lookout for models of beautiful work, powerful work, important work. These examples set the standards for what I and my students aspire to achieve in school. I have a library of work samples, photographs, photocopies, video-tapes, and websites that I draw from and that students draw from when we work

Though it may seem a bit obsessive, documenting these models with the integrity that they deserve is important to us. To make photographic prints or slides of student work at school, we use a professional copy stand and high-quality camera so that the artwork is vivid and true and the writing is bold and legible. When I begin a project with my class by showing slides of impressive student work, I want those slides themselves to fit our standards of quality. When I travel I don't have the luxury of the copy stand, but I photograph work in the best lighting I can, and photocopy work, often in color, as clearly as possible.

In my library I have photographs of historical architectural scale models built by fourth graders in Decatur, Georgia, that would set a high standard even for high school students. I have a field guide to a pond in Dubuque, Iowa, written and illustrated by elementary school students that is bookstore quality. I have blueprints for homes drafted in CAD computer programs by vocational students in Portland, Maine; these blueprints depict houses that were actually built by these students and then sold to families who needed inexpensive homes.

I have note cards created by inner-city middle school students at The Harbor School in Boston depicting islands in Boston Harbor, and note cards by Kindergarten students in Boise, Idaho depicting local birds. Both of these note card sets combine stunning artwork with thoughtful research and writing and are sold in museums and stores.

I have statistical math studies designed by third graders in Maine, exemplary math projects done by elementary students from Texas, and incredible math reflections and explanations written by eighth graders in Cambridge, Massachusetts. I have photocopies of student stories, essays, reviews, and novels and poetry written by students from all over the country.

I have a videotape of public interest television commercials designed and drawn entirely by elementary students in Boston. These ads have aired on commercial television in numerous locations, and they have an innocence and electricity that make them sparkle even to commercial-weary eyes. I have videotapes of original scientific research directed by middle school students in Massachusetts, high school students in Oregon, and elementary students in California. I have videotapes of marginal high school students in Providence, Rhode Island, most of them former dropouts, who have returned to a new internship-based program and are sharing their portfolios of work to a panel. In fact, I have videotapes of portfolio presentations by students from sites all over the country. And I have twenty-five years of models from my own classroom and school—copies, photographs, slides, and videotapes—that I draw from almost daily.

When my class begins a new project, a new venture, we begin with a taste of excellence. I pull out models of work by former students, videotapes of former students presenting their work, models of work from other schools, and models of work from the professional world. We sit and we admire. We critique and discuss what makes the work powerful: what makes a piece of creative writing compelling and exciting; what makes a scientific or historical research project significant and stirring; what makes a novel mathematical solution so breath-taking.

When students arrive at school in the morning they often drift right over to this library of excellence—on the walls, on counters, in boxes—and recharge their vision.

CHAPTER TWO

The First Toolbox
A School Culture of Excellence

Starting Small

IT'S A DARK, RAINY SATURDAY MORNING, ALMOST COLD
enough to snow. I'm driving through the downpour with my lights
on, my truck loaded with boxes of student portfolios and projects,
listening to the windshield wipers, and worrying. The road is almost
empty, just hills and pine trees surround me. My destination is a
small, depressed city with schools that perform miserably. I wonder
again why I agreed to work with this particular school where things
seem so hopeless. What can I possibly offer?

Two hours later I'm sitting in a cluttered, run-down teacher's
room in an ancient brick building. The room smells of stale coffee
and mimeograph fluid. Who uses a mimeograph machine in this
day of photocopiers? I think this but don't say it. The building is
large, in terrible repair; it houses about 1,000 Kindergarten
through fifth grade students. The students are from poor families,
and about half of them do not have English as their first language.
The turnover rate for students is almost 30 percent a year. Each
year the school is judged on the standardized test scores of its students, a third of whom hadn't been in the school the previous year
when the tests were given and half of whom hadn't been in the
school for two years.

Across a battered wooden table sits a well-dressed Latina woman, a special education teacher. She has beautiful eyes and spirit. Though she's been teaching a long time, and, incredibly, in conditions like this, her eyes still have a sparkle. The principal is not at the table. He is in his office and his office is locked. He does not want to meet me and is angry that I am there at all. The teacher apologizes for the principal's rudeness: she knocked on his door, she said, but there was no response.

What was I doing here? The principal doesn't even want me in the building. In half an hour a group of dedicated teachers will come in to meet with me and to share their concerns and questions. I look around at the depressing setting and can't remember why I thought I could be of any support.

I came because this special education teacher wrote a proposal to get some help for the students in her school. She was trapped in a building with an angry principal who had been transferred here after being dismissed from a high school job. He was waiting for retirement; she was waiting for his retirement too. But she was impatient: students needed help now. She was reaching out. When I met her and heard her story, there was no way I could say no. And so I was here, despite the principal. This was the first of our sessions together.

Before the other teachers arrive, I get some background about some of the problems the teachers are facing. I'm overwhelmed. Conditions are so bad that I hardly know what to say. If the teachers were to come in and say they felt like giving up, I would consider them sensible. I feel like giving up myself, right then, apologizing and driving back home in the dark rain. I look at the hopeful eyes of my host and feel a little sick.

When the teachers arrive, I begin by asking them to tell their stories. Not just the war stories, the horror stories, but the stories of what's going well, for which they will have to reach deep: what excites them, what victories they've had. I listen for things we can build on. Then I get out my toolboxes and begin unpacking. Perhaps there are some tools here that can help to build a small change over the next few months. A beginning.

Why Culture Matters

What does *culture* have to do with anything? Schools are for reading, writing, and math. Basic skills. We need to stop wasting our time with all this ridiculous stuff and get back to teaching skills. We're worried about test scores, not culture.

This was how the principal responded when he saw that the written description of my work with teachers was called *Building a Culture of Quality*. I would have liked to have had the opportunity to sit down with that principal and explain that I, too, am worried about performance. That I obsess over basic skills, that I understand the pressure of high-stakes tests, that I care deeply about academic success. To improve these things, culture matters.

The teachers hoped I would have some sort of magic tool in my toolboxes that would make student work improve quickly. Of course I did not, although my toolbox number two, *Work of Excellence,* contains lots of tools I value dearly. Thinking that *projects* or *critique* or *portfolios* are a magic solution to anything is as silly as thinking high-stakes testing will turn schools around. Only as part of a strong classroom culture or school culture are these tools valuable. Culture matters.

I believe the achievement of students is governed to a large degree by their family culture, their neighborhood culture, and their school culture. Students may have different potentials, but, in general, the attitudes and achievements of students are shaped by the culture around them: Students adjust their attitudes and efforts in order to fit into the culture. If the peer culture ridicules academic effort and achievement—it isn't cool to raise your hand in class, to do homework, to care openly about school—this is a powerful force. If the peer culture celebrates investment in school—it's cool to care—this is just as powerful. Schools need to consciously shape their cultures to be places where it's safe to care, where it's cool to care. They need to reach out to family and neighborhood cultures to support this.

Students who attend elite private preparatory schools have an advantage beyond fancy buildings and small class sizes: They have a peer group in which it is normal to spend long hours studying and worrying about academic success. It's normal to pull all nighters, to write long papers, to hope to get into a good college. It's fine to pretend to hate the school or the workload, but it's perfectly normal to work your tail off to get good grades.

Not only at a private school can students have this mindset. Jaime Escalante built his famous calculus program at Garfield High School, a public school with kids from the Los Angeles barrio. He succeeded in part because he was able to transform the norms of the peer culture: Instead of being ridiculed for carrying math books home, his students became heroes who proved to the nation that poor Latino kids can compete with anyone. It wasn't social suicide at Garfield High to admit to spending hours on math homework.

I've had the valuable opportunity of visiting a wide range of schools nationally, elementary and secondary schools, and spending time talking with students about their work and their lives at school. I have a particular interest in understanding what it takes to *fit in*, socially and academically, in different school cultures. I find that students of all ages, from Kindergarten through high school, seem interested in discussing this question. The discussions are generally lively, filled with thoughtful insights and humor. Discussions usually start with the clothing, hairstyles, social behaviors, and musical interests that define acceptance at the school. Then I always push the discussion to include behaviors toward schooling and learning.

An enthusiastic attitude toward learning, made explicit through participating in class discussions and activities and showing excitement for ideas, seems universal in all the Kindergartens I visit across America, whether in poor or wealthy districts. It is *normal* to like school and to say you like school and learning. By secondary school, things are very different in many of the schools I visit.

I am struck in particular by conversations with middle school and high school students from poor urban or rural neighborhoods who attend large schools. When I ask about the social norm for showing interest in school, in learning, in completing homework, I am often met by friendly laughter. Many students related that you would be out of your mind to show interest in school or raise your hand in class. If you want to fit in, you are crazy to let on that you care about your work. This response isn't true of all the students I meet with, but it is a widespread response and is evidenced by most of my classroom visitations. This behavioral norm doesn't seem related to ethnicity – black, white, and Latino students voice this equally – and though the response is more intense from male students, it is voiced by boys and girls alike. It seems in all cases to be a primary obstacle to achievement in these schools.

What if being normal in a school, fitting in, means caring about your work and treating others with respect?

A Classroom Story: The Power of Positive Peer Pressure

I was raised with the message that peer pressure was something terrible, something to avoid, something *negative*. Peer pressure meant kids trying to talk you into smoking cigarettes or taking drugs. I realized after ten years of teaching that *positive* peer pressure was often the primary reason my classroom was a safe, supportive environment for student learning. Peer pressure wasn't something to be afraid of, to be avoided, but rather to be cultivated in a positive direction.

A few years back I got a boy who was new to my school as a sixth grader. He entered the class with a bad attitude and wasn't about to change it to please an adult. The thing I had going for me as a teacher was that underneath his tough exterior he still wanted to fit in.

This boy, whom I'll call Jason, was clear about who he was. The evening of the first day of school I read through his background sheet, an introduction form he had filled out to let me know a bit about his life and interests. Jason had written little, but what he wrote was defensive and angry. I met with him the next day to learn more about him. I learned that Jason's father was a logger who spent his life alone in the woods cutting firewood. Jason worked with him whenever he had the opportunity—clearing brush, stacking wood, cutting, working with heavy equipment. Jason could disassemble, clean and sharpen, and reassemble a chainsaw more efficiently than most adults. He was proud of his skill in the woods and he loved his life in the woods.

Jason hated school, he told me. He hated teachers, he hated schoolwork, and he had always done terribly in school, but it didn't matter. He didn't need school; his father hadn't needed school and he didn't either. Soon he could leave school and cut wood full time and make a living. He hated the fact that he didn't live with his father. He hated the fact that his mother had moved to this junky town. He hated women and girls in general, he said.

Jason made no friends the first two days of school. In the classroom and on the playground he was suspicious and unfriendly. On the third day of school I took the class and their parents on an Outward Bound-type adventure trip to build a sense of community and challenge. We climbed a mountain and went cave exploring together. The students and parents were scared and excited and knew they had to work together as a team. Hours later, covered with mud and scratches and feeling like heroes, we shared hugs and cheers and sandwiches. Jason was a part of the team. Underground, in the dark, he couldn't worry about whose hand he was grabbing for help. He helped others (even girls) and they helped him. He got compliments from others for his support in the tight squeezes and he smiled for the first time.

But he wasn't a new person. The trip had been a beginning, had built important bridges, but back in the classroom it wasn't long before his scowl returned. He'd be darned if he was going to put any effort into his schoolwork.

If my life were a Hollywood movie, I would stand at the black-board (actually a young, handsome movie star version of me would stand at the blackboard) and with brilliant lectures and clever, emotional moments I would transform all the angry Jasons into dedicated, polite students by the sheer power of my personality. I admire the teachers upon whom these movies are based and I don't think these stories are just fairytales. I have to be honest, though, and tell you that it doesn't always work that way. Certainly not for me.

If my teaching personality and spirit were all I had going for me with Jason, I wouldn't have gotten too far. Adult approval was not the big motivator in his life. Fortunately I had the power of the school culture on my side. Students in my school have learned to care since pre-school. They have shared their work with pride since they were four years old to different audiences. They have been surrounded by models of strong work and children who enjoy school, care about their work, and are outspoken about it. They have learned to feel that a safe and inclusive emotional environment is the norm. This is not to say that work or behavior is always good but rather that it is expected. To fit in, in this school, working hard and treating people well is expected.

There was no role for a mean-spirited class clown in our classroom. Jason may have garnered social power and attention in other schools by cracking jokes at the expense of others or at the expense of class lessons, but here he got only frustration and complaints from peers. Jason may have fit in fine in other schools by turning in lousy work—it might have even helped his credibility with the boys—but here he was met with critical eyes and helpful suggestions from peers.

Unlike the Hollywood version, the turning point for Jason came not after an inspirational lecture I gave nor a tough, heart-to-heart talk I had with him after school. It came when he first took the risk to care about his work and was met with enthusiasm and encouragement from peers. Jason put almost no effort into his schoolwork, and he received feedback from peers during critique sessions that was not unkind but was critical. When Jason turned in sloppy, meager work, other students advised him to put a little more care into it. He met their suggestions with defensive anger.

The first time Jason pinned up something for class critique that was well done, he was showered with compliments from the class: They knew what a breakthrough this was for him. He actually blushed, despite the fact that much of the positive feedback was from girls, whom he was supposed to hate. In the same way, the first time Jason stepped out of his role as a bully to do something nice for another student, it was discussed during our morning meeting and he was met with unfamiliar praise.

During the course of the fall Jason's work began to improve along with his attitude. At first when he turned in careless papers he said he didn't care. When I edited his work with him he argued. Later, when he began to enjoy some positive feedback from classmates, he grew less resistant to my suggestions. At one point he looked at his work and smiled. I'm proud of this, he said. I think it's the first good thing I've ever really done in school. *I think the class will like this.*

At our January Exhibition Night, Jason had a table. The project he was sharing—each student completed a project—was one in which he had invented a character and wrote a file and a book documenting this character's life. Each student had created a different character. Jason drew a portrait of this person and wrote a physical description, a personality description, a family description, a career description, and a life history. He prepared family trees and created realistic artifacts from his character's life: birth certificate, adoption papers, diploma, credit cards, letters, newspaper articles, police records, business documents. He created the financial artifacts of this character: paychecks, checking and savings account books, investment portfolios, tax forms, loan records, and insurance forms. He drafted scale blueprints of the home he had designed for his character. His table and the display board next to it represented his months of work and he obsessed all afternoon about arranging it perfectly.

Jason's character was a crusty old logger. Though his face was weathered and tired, his hands battered and scarred, his eyes were clear. He was past retirement age but never considered leaving the woods. Jason's book sat on a bed of fresh wood chips, cut the day before and filling the room with the sweet aroma of oak. The book leaned against a chainsaw and was framed by plastic cans of bar oil and gasoline and Jason's model of a skidder carrying miniature logs. Jason stood with pride as classmates directed their parents over to his table: You've got to read Jason's family description, they said. The whole class loved it.

Jason's academic skills didn't become stellar overnight and his personality remained difficult at times. He was often resistant to receiving help right up until his graduation. But he was a different kid. He made eye contact with me and with others. He was proud of his work. He was willing to put time into reading and writing. *He had bought in to school.* He was willing to treat others, even girls, respectfully.

I saw Jason recently while out on a run early one Saturday morning. I was ten miles into the run, lost in thought on a woodland road, when I was startled by a yell from the forest. Hey, Mr. B! How you doing? I stopped and saw a larger Jason, his hand bandaged from a logging accident, dragging brush from the woods. He couldn't shake my hand due to the bandages but he gave me a respectful nod. He was still in school—high school now—and we talked about his life. Before I left he looked at me and said, That was a pretty good character file I did in sixth grade, huh? I bet you never had a character like that before. No I haven't, I said. I still show slides of your project to students when they're starting character files. He nodded with pride.

The Value of Community

Where do you begin to rebuild the culture?, the teachers asked. How do you start?

There is no easy answer or correct answer to this. In a culture where much has to change it is difficult to say there is one correct place to begin. My personal passion is a culture built around beautiful student work, so I always feel inclined to begin with the work. But every school is different, with different needs. In many schools it's almost impossible to address issues of work until fundamental issues of physical safety, emotional safety, respect, and courtesy are addressed, or issues of size, scheduling, and communication are dealt with.

One thing clear to me though is that the power of the culture rests in community. When I've visited effective schools I've been struck with the realization that though the settings and resources are often widely different, every effective school I've seen has a strong sense of community. I've seen this in elite residential private schools and in successful inner-city programs for former school dropouts. Students and staff in all these settings feel that they are a part of something—they belong to something.

My Carnegie Foundation colleague Jason Raley has been researching a tiny high school that has attracted local and national recognition for taking high-risk urban students and sending 100 precent of them on to college. Articles on the school have showcased its tough standards and its curriculum as the reason for its success. These factors are doubtless critical, but Jason found another factor which seemed to be foremost in student minds. They felt safe there. Not just physically safe, but safe to take risks, safe to care about trying hard. They felt supported as part of a community. The students and teachers I've met from Central Park East High School, Urban Academy in New York, The Fenway in Boston—all small high schools with similar remarkable records of reversing the trend of low achievement for urban students of color to one of high graduation rates and college acceptance levels—stress the sense of community as the core of school success.

A strong spirit of community in a school can do much more than help college acceptance statistics. Each spring I drive across the state to attend a performance of a student play at the Graham and Parks School in Cambridge, Massachusetts. My friend Kathy Greeley, a seventh- and eighth-grade humanities teacher, manages somehow to guide her students each year in the writing and production of an incredible piece of theater, a play that is the culmination of their historical studies. The students are black and white, Haitian, Latino, Asian American; their backgrounds, languages, and accents differ. Each year they overcome their differences to write and produce an historical play that leaves the audience in tears, and each year as the play concludes they gather together on the stage with pride in celebration of their multiracial community. Kathy's book *Why Fly That Way? Linking Community and Academic Achievement* documents one year in the life of her classroom, culminating with such a play. The community they built did more than raise academic standards: Her students became better people. Building the classroom community strengthened the character of students to make them more thoughtful, polite, honest, and courageous individuals. They moved a long way toward becoming the type of citizens we wish for in society.

I've been fortunate to work with The Eagle Rock School, a

wilderness high school in Colorado for students whom the world has given up on: After multiple expulsions, truancy, drugs, and often jail, these kids aren't wanted anywhere. The school has a tightly knit community that works day and night to support and direct students. Not all students make it to college or even graduation, but the transformation in the character of students is remarkable. The new students are sullen and angry. The veteran students are polite, responsible, open, and honest; they lead school tours with warmth, humor, and pride; they baby-sit the children of the teachers; they care for the buildings and grounds.

Two other schools in which I've done consultation work are urban schools with a focus on community and character: Newsome Park Elementary in Newport News, Virginia, and The Harbor School, a middle school in Boston. Both schools are in city choice programs and both are in rough neighborhoods that would ordinarily have trouble attracting students. The strong community focus at both of these sites has earned them reputations for safety and personal attention. Last year The Harbor School was the most requested middle school in Boston, and Newsome Park had a waiting list of 1600 students.

Building strong school communities means fighting the social trend of bigger everything, the trend of super-stores and massive shopping malls. Deborah Meier points out that in education, the notion that "bigger is better" is entirely wrong. In a small school students and teachers are highly accountable—it's hard for the student to fall through the cracks. The web of personal relationships supports and pushes students and staff. Decisions can be made without consulting a giant and cumbersome bureaucracy. In a small district administrators are highly accountable and communication is constant.

In rural settings around my home and around the country, state legislatures and departments of education decided that small-town kids were being denied the giant gymnasiums, swimming pools, and varied language courses found at large schools. Plus, small schools weren't cost effective. So they were closed and students were bused far away to large, impersonal regional buildings. The schools that were shut down were places where almost every student was in the school play, the school orchestra, the school athletic teams. Everyone was involved. Now, because discipline and dropout problems are up and academic performance is down, it doesn't seem like closing those schools was such a good idea after all. The loss of community brought on by the "bigger is better" mentality is evolving as a painful chapter for American education.

There is at least some movement now to downsize: Many districts are now working to establish smaller schools—charters, pilots, schools within a school. Many large high schools are breaking down into separate houses or teams, or using strategies to make things more human: limiting the number of students that each teacher sees; assigning students to a small advisory group for multiple years; giving students a mentor from the professional world outside of school or from the faculty or student body; employing student focus groups, student panels, or peer mediators to address problems.

When considering how to improve education for children, people tend to focus on what's being delivered to students, and how to refine the package. I think it's more useful to consider schooling not as a delivery system but as an experience. What does a student go through in the course of a day? How does a student behave in this school in order to fit in? Where do students feel safe? What are the opportunities for the student to contribute, to create, and to be recognized for his or her talents or efforts? What motivates a student to care? This exercise is particularly powerful if the focus is a marginal student, one whose race, background, or academic or physical needs label him or her different, therefore out of the mainstream.

America's schools, particularly our high schools, have large groups of students who feel that school is just not a place that works for them. Penny Eckert points out in her book *Jocks and Burnouts* that while popular, successful students learn assimilation to society in school, it's a very different story for others. Those students who don't buy in to the school experience learn alienation and resentment which often follow them all their lives. These students are not going to be captured by new state standards or new tests. They need a school community that brings them into the fold and pushes and supports them to succeed.

Building a Foundation for Community

I worked briefly with a school in inner city Boston. The building was surrounded by trash: fast-food boxes, plastic bags, food, broken bottles, wet newspapers, shopping carts, and needles from drug users. People sat on the curb in front of the school drinking from paper bags; the liquor store was across the street. The building had the architectural look of a prison—massive exterior walls of water-stained concrete with few windows. The front entrance was a battered metal door covered with graffiti; if you banged loudly enough they would buzz you in for inspection by a security guard. The boy's bathrooms had stalls with no doors, broken toilet seats, and graffiti on the walls and metal mirrors.

This was an elementary school. A thousand young children went to this school, including seven Kindergarten classes. Imagine your five-year-old son or daughter walking to this place every morning. If politicians or business leaders were compelled to send their own children to this school, I would guess we'd see changes in the building fairly soon.

And these schools are not just in cities. I spent ten minutes standing in front of a school in rural Arkansas, just staring. The grounds were tattered with dry dirt mounds, tall weeds, and trash. The building was dirty cinderblock with no windows. The plastic school sign next to me on the state highway was broken and crooked. If this was your place of business, could you imagine bringing a client here and inspiring any confidence about the quality of work going on inside? Are parents and children less important than business clients?

Architects point out that it's easy to see what is valued in a culture by looking at which structures are built with expense and care, such as the pyramids of ancient Egypt and Latin America, the temples of ancient Greece and Rome, the castles of Europe and China, and the elaborate cathedrals of Europe. These structures were built to protect or honor their Gods and their kings. Today our architectural temples honor business: the skyscrapers of the world are all commercial buildings. When kids walk into run-down, ugly buildings constructed as cheaply as possible and often falling apart, what message do these children get? We don't care about you. We don't value you. We don't expect much of you.

When families look at such schools in their community how can they have hope? Newspapers may cry out about low test scores and state officials may mandate more retention of students, but everyone who lives near dirty, dilapidated schools knows where the problems begin. Schools for wealthy children certainly don't look like this.

Two friends of mine, Margarita Munez, a principal in Roxbury, Massachusetts, and Sylvia Garza, a principal in San Antonio, Texas, each inherited buildings that were in terrible physical condition. Each refused to live with it. They were angry and determined, and they reached out to the community for help. By pressuring the district, raising funds, transferring custodial staff, and gathering volunteer help from parents, teachers and community members, these two women transformed their buildings: things were repaired, repainted, remodeled, and kept sparkling clean.

Walking into Garza's Douglas School in San Antonio, the neighborhood looked every bit as poor as the neighborhood of the Boston school building described earlier. This school was a different story. It was not only clean but also inviting. The entry was cheerfully decorated with live plants, a rug, banners, and a welcoming easel holding friendly messages. Students entered this school smiling and greeted me with polite pride. When I was given a tour of the building by third graders, they couldn't wait to boast about all the changes in the past year. Doesn't this look great?!, they remarked with a grin at every turn. On the tour we entered a large room in a back building that looked like a store for used clothing. My guides informed me that these clothes were donated and were free to be used by anyone in the school anytime; sometimes kids come to school without shoes or coats, they explained.

A few years ago I had the opportunity to visit schools in the Gaza Strip, Palestinian schools funded by the United Nations. Squeezed into a tiny old car, I was driven through a maze of broken streets littered with pipes and building debris, crowded with donkeys and barefoot children. Through enormous refugee camps we twisted and turned until we stopped in a narrow dirt alley at a tattered gate. My guide yelled something in Arabic and the gate was opened; we drove into a sea of children on a dirt playground, children who pressed their faces against the car windows. I emerged from the car and looked around, amazed. The physical grounds showed meticulous care. The cinderblock walls were painted white and covered with giant murals of flowers. Shrubs and rose bushes were carefully groomed and a team of little students was sweeping the sidewalks where I stood. This school had no money to spare—it had triple sessions during the day just to squeeze in the local children, and still classes of first graders averaged about 60 pupils, few of whom had supplies. Yet they took pride in their place of learning.

A clean and well-kept building guarantees nothing about the quality of work children will accomplish within it. But it matters. It's a message. It's a visual model of the ethic within the building. The building doesn't have to be a palace—my visit to schools in Gaza made this very clear—but it has to show the children, the teachers, and the parents that somebody cares about them. I don't think this is possible without local pride. When a community is proud of its schools the children who live there become part of this ethic. If the pride is absent, even renovations and improvements are soon covered with graffiti or are vandalized.

The same is true for the quality of learning within the building. Kindergartners are excited to go to school and learn in almost any conditions; older students are quickly sensitized to the reputation of the school. If the local community—the families, the businesses, the kids on the streets—see a school as a good one, a positive environment, a ticket to a better life, students get the message that it makes sense to *try* there. When success at the school is valued in the community it give students a reason to care.

I was struck by an unusually clear example of the power of local community pride when reading H.G. Bissinger's *Friday Night Lights*, a story of a high school football season in Odessa, Texas. What the town valued in the school flourished.

Odessa took pride in football. The town raised money to build an enormous stadium for the Permian High School football team. The building seats almost 20,000; it has an artificial-surface field sunken 18 feet below ground level, a two-story press box with VIP seating for school board members and dignitaries, and a full-time caretaker who lived at the stadium. In 1988 the team spent over $70,000 that year on travel expenses because they used a chartered jet to attend games. On Fridays—game days—much of the town went to work dressed in black, the team color. Friday nights, while the towns-people filed into the stadium, the players walked in to the locker room to see their new uniforms freshly ironed and helmets brightly polished by boosters. The school quarterback had a billboard erected on his lawn for the season by the booster club. The Permian football team had been dominant for generations; it was the most successful team in Texas football history.

The town didn't take the same pride in other aspects of schooling. Academics was so much on the back burner that the entire budget for the school's English Department was less than the football team's budget for game videos. Test scores were low; college acceptances were low also. For boys the only road to community respect was football.

For girls things were perhaps worse. The ultimate status in the girl's social world of Permian High was to become a "Pepette," a personal booster assigned to a member of the football team. The Pepettes decorated the players' lockers, baked them cakes and cookies, embroidered pillows for them, made them scrapbooks, wrote them encouraging letters, and celebrated them with banners and special prizes. Academic achievement was risky. As Julie Gardner, a student at Permian, explained in the book, "You couldn't be too smart. You had to act silly or they put you in a category right away. It was the end of your social life if you were an intelligent girl." Not a single girl in the high school in 1988 had an SAT score above 650 in either math or language.

This story fascinated me. Look at what happened when an entire town came together to support a school. I'm not against school sports; I attend games regularly and spent many years coaching. But I began to imagine: What if the town's vision of excellence was not centered just on football? What if some of the millions spent on the new stadium had been used to build a giant, state-of-the-art library and media center with scores of computers, a beautiful theater and television studio, new science labs, darkrooms and art studios? What if thousands of citizens turned out on Friday nights to see student theater or dance or exhibitions of student projects? What if all the town boosters who donated time and money to keep the football team flourishing were donating their time and money as school boosters: mentors, tutors, guest teachers, volunteers in the building? What if the students who were Merit Scholars and arts award recipients, the students who won math competitions or got accepted at colleges, were celebrated in town with banners or headlines in the paper, with attention and status? It's just a dream but it really got me thinking.

At the same time as H.G. Bissinger was writing the story of Permian High School in Odessa, Texas, something very different was going on in Fort Worth. The Morningside Middle School had a new principal, Odessa Ravin. Facing a desperate situation of poverty and crime surrounding the school, she reached out to a local business alliance. With help from businesses, churches, and the neighborhood, the school and the alliance together turned things around. This was the birth of the network of Alliance Schools, now known throughout Texas and the country. Tom Hatch, in his *Education Leadership* article of May 1998, "How Community Contributes to Achievement," describes how this small beginning in Morningside grew to a network of over 100 Alliance Schools, all committed to engaging the community to help with education. The results, measured in test scores or community safety, are a national model.

Supporting Community Inside and Out

Compared to building a community, building a house is easy. If you build it well, it won't need maintenance for years. Building and maintaining a positive community takes constant vigilance. Like raising young children, it's a job that's never really done. Frequently, it's discouraging or overwhelming. To have a quality school, however, I don't think there's any choice—it takes attention always, and lots of it. The staff at my school commits a tremendous amount of time to this endeavor, time that doesn't fit neatly into state mandates of "time on learning" or curriculum labels. I believe it is time well spent.

I always describe my teaching situation as privileged, but it is not a privilege of affluence. At its core this privilege is simply a freedom to build a culture well. Because my school is located a bit in the middle of nowhere—we're a one-school district—we the staff have been trusted with the responsibility of making most of the important decisions about educating our students based on what we see works best. We don't have salaries or material budgets that would make anyone jealous, but we have earned the trust of the community to shape our school.

Many school staffs have little or no say in how their building is organized, how their day is organized, how money is spent, who is hired, what is taught, how it is taught, and what the goals and vision of the school should be. They have no ownership beyond their individual classroom or office and so feel powerless to deal with broad issues of school culture and communication, or with issues of general student achievement and character. I am fortunate to work with a staff that feels ownership for the school as a whole, and through constant and difficult meetings works to keep the school on a good course. We have an active voice in all of these decisions, and we take this responsibility seriously. We have dedicated our lives to it.

When I arrived at my school twenty-five years ago, the new building was controversial in town. It was a modest cinderblock structure but was considered by many in town to be enormous and extravagant. It had a gym/cafeteria, a library, and a full-time principal. Why, just a few years back the town got by with a two-room wooden schoolhouse for all the children; how could we possibly need all this *stuff?* But the population had grown, and we could no longer get by with two teachers for all of the students in the town. When I arrived, I was one of five teachers. Two of those five teachers, Bob Dihlmann and Ken Lindsay, are still working at the school with me twenty-five years later. None of us have become rich financially but we've dedicated our lives to this school in exchange for a different type of wealth.

The long-term commitment of the staff is a testament to the honor of being trusted to chart our course. Over the years I've worked with ten different principals at this school but few teachers have left. Ordinarily such changes in leadership undermine a school culture, with each new building administrator trying to tug the school in a different direction. In our case things were different. A visionary superintendent stayed in his post for twenty-five years and supported a hiring process in which the staff had an integral voice in hiring new teachers and new principals. Because of this, we were graced with a series of strong administrators who shared our vision of the school and added to its growth, and we were able to hire teachers who welcomed our different approach to schooling.

We worked hard in the early days to win the support of a skeptical town community. We still do. Along with our local control comes a high level of accountability, which I respect. We have no mayor in town; decisions are made at open town meetings where all the citizens of the town can gather and look at the town budget together. My neighbors sit next to me at town meeting and, after discussing whether the town can afford to buy a used pick-up truck for road maintenance, read a handout listing my personal salary on it, and detailing how every penny of the school budget is to be spent. If we want the citizens of the town to approve our budget, we need to convince them all year that we're doing a good job, that we can be trusted. This trust can't be built only on test scores. People in town are wise enough to know that there's a lot more to life than scores; they have higher standards than this. They want their children to be polite and kind and responsible, to treat others well. They want them to value hard work and quality work. They want their children to love school, to love reading and writing, math and science, history.

We have built into our school culture a number of structures to foster these qualities in children, structures we have borrowed from a wide range of educational sources. These structures are at the core of our curriculum, yet would not be found in most curriculum lists and would not even be allowed in some schools.

We honor children with a great deal of responsibility and we expect them to live up to this honor. Rather than seeing school as something being done to them, students are given the responsibility to carry out original academic projects, save work in portfolios, display their work, and reflect publicly on their work and their learning. They present their work regularly in school assemblies and in exhibitions for the town community. They give school tours which center on the work we do, and they undertake projects to help the town in many different ways.

Every older student in the school is paired with a younger student as a helper, tutor, and guide. Graduation speeches of sixth graders often refer to how they were helped as a Kindergartner by their older buddy, and how they were able to return this gift as an older buddy themselves. It's not uncommon for a little face to poke into my fifth- and sixth-grade classroom and ask, with a sad or worried voice, Can I see my buddy for a minute?

Students work in the cafeteria, set up for events, shovel snow, clean up school grounds, help the school custodian and, every day, clean up their classrooms. During lunch and recess, many older students help direct the younger students in gym or art classes. For many years, students replaced the school secretary when she was absent, answering the phone and taking messages to teachers. Service is considered an active part of citizenship.

We are a school of meetings. Instead of being isolated in classrooms all the time, teachers continually meet in teams and as a whole faculty to build and monitor our curriculum and to maintain a good tone to the building. Our teaching schedule has been organized to allow for, and to support, this type of collaboration. We try to model the cooperation and teamwork that we expect from children. Our staff meetings are rarely easy and fun: though we share a similar vision for the school, we argue about every detail along the way. Nevertheless, we have been trusted to run the school together, and the students see clearly that we respect and support each other.

Every classroom day opens with a morning meeting in which the teacher and the children sit in a circle and begin together. It is a time to go over the schedule for the day and to take attendance, but importantly it is a time to set the right tone for school for every child, to establish a positive and polite emotional environment for learning. We take time to explicitly teach the traditions of courtesy—manners—and we take time every morning to reinforce the value of respect. We often review the previous day's highlights or problems with behavior and learning, and commit ourselves to a constructive day together. Children are given a chance to share from their home life; if there are joyful or tragic stories from home, morning meeting is a safe environment for students to let their peers and teacher know about them. In addition to morning meetings, students meet regularly with their grade level teams and with the school as a whole, both to share work and to work at maintaining a school that is polite and safe for all students—physically safe and emotionally safe.

We regularly reach out to the community around us. Town citizens of all ages are in the school every day as mentors and tutors for children. Senior citizens are hosted for concerts, for annual Valentine and Thanksgiving meals hosted by the Kindergarten and Pre-Kindergarten. We invite town citizens to our work exhibitions, to be panelists at formal portfolio presentations, and as experts, helping our classes in their learning. Students clean town roads every year, raise money for town efforts, and engage in other serious projects to benefit the community: testing homes for radon, testing streams for pollution, testing wells for water quality, conducting research to contribute to town historical records, taking a census of local animals for state officials. It's not by chance that we've earned trust and support for the school.

The level of this support was particularly evident to me a few years back when we needed to remodel our building. We were compelled to move the entire contents of the school to a derelict school building we rented in a nearby town during the year-long renovation. Rather than hire a moving company, the town citizens simply pitched in, like at a barn raising, with dozens of pick-up trucks, old station wagons, and construction vans being put into service. While some families made coffee and sandwiches, others loaded cars. When the move was done, families helped paint and repair the rented building, working along with teachers.

That year area towns made an effort to get our town to join a new regional district in order to bring in state funds. The school staff was worried: We didn't want to lose our autonomy and become part of a big bureaucracy; we didn't want to lose what we had built so carefully. But it was out of our hands: it was to be a town meeting vote. With the school closed for repairs, the townspeople gathered one evening in the volunteer fire shed, crowded in the garage with heavy rain pounding on the metal roof. In an unusual show of unity, the town citizens were of one mind on this issue. It may be a different kind of school we have here, said one older man, but it's *our* school. And it works! Kids love school in this town! They can't take that away from us. Of the 220 voters crowded in the garage, less than ten voted to regionalize. I stood with tears in my eyes.

A Classroom Story:
Building a Broad Notion of Community

I'm sitting in a bus headed for New York City on a slushy January morning. There are snow flurries in the air but the early morning sun is emerging and it pierces the foggy bus windows. The bus is filled with small town folks in muddy winter jackets—students and parents from my school. Many have never been to a city this size. The parents chat quietly; the students are too excited and nervous to sit still. To reach excellence in education you need to start with some inspiration and excitement. We have a bus full of it here.

Despite their energy many of my students are silent: They communicate with their friends this morning in American Sign Language (A.S.L.). In four hours they will be paired with Deaf students in Manhattan who use no voice at all. The signing that they do now is last-minute preparation.

None of my students is Deaf but as a class we are engaged in a deep study of Deaf culture. Because neither I nor my family is a part of this culture, I have been able to plan and orchestrate this study only through the generous help of the local Deaf community and my Deaf friends. As a class, we've studied the history of the Deaf both internationally and nationally and have studied the political movement for Deaf rights. We've read literature with Deaf characters and created Deaf characters for our writing. With assistance from a university laboratory researching communication disorders, we've studied the physics of sound and the anatomy and physiology of the ear and hearing. My students can read audiograms and explain the medical and social issues of cochlear implants and hearing aids; they've interviewed people who diagnose hearing problems, people who prescribe aids and implants, people who wear aids and implants, and people vehemently opposed to both. From hosting a series of Deaf guests of different ages and backgrounds students have learned about the culture itself—the different sense of values, time, relationships, manners, humor, and life priorities that distinguish this culture from hearing cultures. With the help of our guests, videotapes, books, and class lessons, students have gained a beginning competency in A.S.L.

The greatest achievement of the study so far has not actually been the work—though there's been excellent work—but rather the level of understanding of the Deaf culture that we've reached. Our discussions and informal debates have been constant, deep, and inspiring. Meeting Deaf people on opposite sides of every controversial issue for the Deaf—oralism versus signing, A.S.L. versus Sign English, mainstreaming versus Deaf institutions, day programs v.

residential schools, cochlear implants v. acceptance of deafness—students have been confused and torn over what is right, what is just, what is ethical. The more they've learned and the more people they've met, the messier the issues and the debates have become. Students developed rigid opinions of right and wrong early in our study, and then came face to face with people who didn't fit their vision and stereotypes. Nothing was black and white anymore. It's been terrific.

The core of the study has been the personal contact. The pressure on students has been intense and not because they are worried about tests. We have had tests, but the big worries are because we are continually hosting Deaf guests and visiting Deaf communities. It's one thing to study a new language for a test and quite another to study because you know you'll soon be in the middle of the culture, trying to understand, trying to be polite, trying to build bridges of friendship. My students have been begging for more knowledge; they practice sign during recess and after school.

Two of my colleagues, Penny Gill and Kathy Kurtz, planned this unit of study with me. Both have taught in schools for the Deaf and they used their contacts to help establish partnerships between our students and students in various schools for the Deaf. We've spent time in an oral school that uses speech and no sign at all, a total communication school that uses speech and sign both, and a bilingual-bicultural school that uses A.S.L. almost exclusively and teaches written English as a second language. The school we are visiting today is a particularly Deaf environment. The principal is Deaf; much of the teaching and support staff is Deaf, even the security guards sign. We are preparing to enter a different world, and my students are nervous. So am I.

Staring out of the bus window, my doubts and fears start to take over. This could be a disaster. No large group of hearing children has visited this school in anyone's memory. The Deaf community in general is protective of its fragile culture and often suspicious of hearing intrusions; most schools for the Deaf I've approached were not open to a visit—they didn't know me or trust me. They pictured a crowd of hearing kids walking through their halls gawking at their students, and nothing I communicated to them put them at ease. It's a miracle that I was able to gain access to this wonderful school; I still can't believe they agreed to this visit when I have no close friends or contacts in the building. I visited the school in December and the principal and teachers were gracious and kind, but I'm not sure how clear the arrangements were left with staff members. It's possible that things could be confusing and disorganized when we arrive and even possible that students in the school will be mistrustful and hostile when they see a big crowd of white hearing people in their hallways.

I spend some time this morning with two fifth-grade girls, Sonia and Lisa, to engage in some signed conversation and regain my confidence about the trip. I'll be depending on these girls today. They are strong signers and socially confident and outgoing. I know if anyone is going to reach out and break the ice today to begin relationships with the Deaf students, these two girls will be the ones who take the lead. I need a little of their positive spirit right now.

My fears of disaster are well founded. The bus stops on a busy street in lower Manhattan and the students and parents emerge overwhelmed into the chaos of crowds, steam, and racket. They look up, gawking at the giant buildings as pedestrians push their way through and divide our ranks; with the traffic noise my directions are impossible to hear. Once I manage to get everyone inside the building there's no one to greet us and the security guard is confused by our presence; we're sent downstairs to a dim basement cafeteria to wait for our hosts. The cafeteria is crowded with high school kids who tower over us, mostly African American students horsing around with typical teenage rowdiness. It's noisier than a cafeteria in a hearing school—a fact that startles and surprises the parents in my group. A crowd of curious Deaf students surrounds us and the questions come flying in sign, too fast to understand. My students and parents look like they're in shock, huddled together and too timid to sit down. As I try to initiate some communication, Lisa pushes her way through the crowd to try to explain to these high school students what this strange white crowd is doing in their building. Finally, familiar faces of teachers and fifth- and sixth-grade students appear, people I'd met in December, and we retreat upstairs to begin school tours. It's clear to me that this day is out of my control. I can only pray that it goes well.

The Deaf student hosts are wonderful: They welcome us and introduce themselves and are patient with the speed of our signing. They split us into small groups, and before I know it my students and parents have all disappeared. For almost two hours I wander through the building, worried, but each time I stumble on a tour group the group is happily engaged observing or participating in a class. The guides are full of warmth and pride in showing their school, and even the parents from my group seem relaxed and included. The teachers in the school are welcoming everywhere.

Eventually I relax enough to join one tour group working with preschoolers in a small room. The group is led by a tall, elegant African American girl, a sixth grader. She leads us with grace and smiles. She answers adult questions with unusual maturity (my students voice and sign interpret for their parents) and is playful with my students, teasing them in friendly ways and breaking into cartwheels in the gymnasium.

At the end of the day, relaxing and eating cookies together in a crowded, sunny classroom, no one wants to leave. There are photographs and hugs and promises to stay in touch. The promises are kept.

After exchanging letters and videotapes all spring, the students in both schools hatch a plan to have the New York students come up to Massachusetts for an overnight visit where they will stay in student homes. The New York school bureaucracy makes this close to impossible, but heroic teachers at the School for the Deaf manage to get district and parental permission and line up a bus, and the principal gives them his blessing.

For weeks my classroom is suffused with excited planning. My students are consumed with discussions of how to be good hosts. What do we feed them? Where do we take them? How do we make sure they're comfortable in a small town in the woods when few of these students have left New York City in their lives?

The class decides to send delegates to each of the other classrooms in the school to explain about our guests—to tell them what to expect and how to make our visitors feel welcome. They understand that a big group of visiting kids, all of whom are non-white and Deaf, will be just as startling to the younger kids in our school as we were to kids in New York. The younger students are excited and listen intently. My students also agree to teach their parents the basics of politeness in Deaf culture so that our guests will feel comfortable staying overnight in a strange place. They agree to watch over our guests carefully; unlike usual sleepovers where parents can do most of the work of making sure the guest kids are comfortable, the hosting responsibilities will be almost entirely on my students because their parents don't sign. The students are so excited they can talk of little else for weeks. I'm so nervous that I email my Deaf friend Karen Glickman across the state and ask if she'll come stay with my family for a few days to help me manage the visit. She agrees.

When the students finally arrive we host a luncheon banquet in the classroom, thanks to parent help, and Karen does a presentation to the students about her life with Delta, her hearing guide dog. We spend much of the afternoon at the farm of Bobby, one of my students, feeding cows, feeding fish in the pond, playing with the dogs, drinking juice together. Spending time with animals, something my students take for granted, is exciting, overwhelming, for the New York kids. They are entranced by the cows and panicked by the mosquitoes and black flies. And they love the dogs. (Two of the deaf boys who are staying over at a girl's house that evening, ended up waking at five o'clock the next morning so they could play with the family dog before breakfast.) We visit a local waterfall, play on the rocks and in the swirling water and everyone gets soaked and silly together.

Overnight visits go well—the next morning it takes an hour to share all the sleepover stories. One small Deaf boy was told by his host, a sixth-grade girl, that he could choose a toy to sleep with if he wished. The toy he chose turned out to have a motion-activated siren that screeched all night every time he rolled over in bed. My student was so happy he was sleeping well that she didn't have the heart to wake him and tell him about the siren.

There was a moment on this visit, after our pizza dinner party in the park of a nearby town, when we were walking down a small-town street at sunset toward the ice cream parlor. The students were walking on the sidewalk with their arms around each other, the girls holding hands and skipping. Black, Hispanic, Asian, and white kids, Deaf and hearing, city and country. I walked behind them and I thought about just how lucky I was. This was a scene that would not have been possible in my youth. I felt lucky just to be there to see it, to be a part of it.

We spent the second day at school where our guests met the younger students and spent time with our Kindergarten buddies. When their bus finally loaded up in front of the school to leave, there were lots of tears from kids and adults too. Even Jeremy, the biggest, toughest boy in their class, a handsome African American basketball player, pointed silently through the bus window at my Jeremy, a big white basketball player, his new friend, and they both had tears in their eyes.

This is as good an example as any of what I'm striving for in education. I'm as proud of this study as any I've done. Unfortunately it has no place in the narrow blueprint for schooling being proposed by so many individuals today. Much of what my students learned in this study is not in the new prescriptive state curriculum "standards." Little of what we learned will make my students better test takers. Few teachers are given the latitude to stray from required textbooks and schedules to attempt this type of teaching. There's no time in the new "standards" for a deep investigation of culture.

The gains my students made may not show up on standardized tests but they were very real. These students will never again view history and science without ethical questions and discerning eyes; they will hunger for deep intellectual discussion and debate; they will be open to understanding different customs and cultures; they will have the memory of a friendship that transcended race and background; they will have the proud memory of being a part of one of the greatest of human endeavors: showing kindness in hosting and caring for others. This study built a spirit of inquiry and excellence that I hope will stay alive in their hearts. It modeled a vision of culture founded in respect. It expanded the notion of excellence to include excellence as a human being—being the kind of person who will be a credit to our society.

CHAPTER THREE

The Second Toolbox
Work of Excellence

Self-Esteem from Accomplishments, not Compliments

ANOTHER SATURDAY, BACK AT THE SCHOOL OF THE ANGRY principal. He's not in the building today; things are more calm and relaxed. Despite his threats to discipline or transfer teachers who undermined "the direction of the school," he seems to have been too busy or too distracted to make life difficult for the group of teachers here. I've never even met him. No one in the group has given up yet.

It's a gray winter day, giant piles of dirty snow in the parking lot, snow dripping down from the roof outside the windows. There's a white five-gallon bucket on the teacher's room counter catching drips leaking from the ceiling. We can hear the drip, drip, drip as we meet.

The power of community is starting to kick in for us. This is a small group of teachers—just twelve—from a giant staff, but that's not such a bad thing. We've gotten to know each other. Not just me meeting the staff, but the staff getting to know and support each other. In this building of closed doors, the teamwork in our group is a new and welcome thing.

We're a mixed group of regular education teachers, bilingual teachers, special education teachers, and part-time administrators.

Other than me, the group is all women, but ages and backgrounds vary widely. About half the teachers are more comfortable with Spanish than English, and the other half feel the opposite way. What we have in common is our mission together along with a small grant from the state that can be used to pay for curriculum materials and supplies. The group is very proud of this grant.

I have no illusions regarding bringing about a major transformation in this school, nor does the group. We're starting small with our effort and it may stay small. But there's some hope in the room today.

Since meeting with me on Saturdays, the group has begun to meet regularly during the week, and each member has paired off with another to give advice and support. Teachers have been working together to plan curriculum and projects, and especially to combine classes. The state grant is called an *inclusion grant*. Its purpose is to support special education students and bilingual students to be included more often in regular education classrooms.

I'm pleased to say that this has already begun. Bridges are being built between groups of students who were isolated in the past. The teachers are very pleased that some of the initial collaborative work has succeeded. They expected the mainstream students to be tough on the special education and Spanish-speaking students, but this hasn't been the case at all—instead they've been welcoming. The seeds of a new culture are sprouting, at least in one part of the building.

As a group, we've built a safe environment for sharing. Now we can get down to the heart of my consultation: looking at student work. This will be a little painful at first.

The teachers are protective and defensive of their students. The students' work is not very good, they say, but they are struggling. Their lives are so hard, they move from home to home so often, their skills are shaky, they have no confidence. Before they can do strong work, the teachers explain, we have to build their self-esteem.

I'm pleased that the teachers are sympathetic to their students but I explain that I have a different perspective. We can't *first* build the students' self-esteem and *then* focus on their work. *It is through their own work that their self-esteem will grow.* I don't believe self-esteem is built from compliments. Students who are struggling or producing lousy work know exactly how poor their performance is—compliments never seem genuine. All the self-esteem activities and praise in the world won't make them feel like proud students until they do something they can value.

When they begin to make discoveries that impress their classmates, solve problems as part of the group, put together projects that are admired by others, produce work of real quality, a new self-image as a proud student will emerge.

It's time to take out my biggest toolbox and talk about strategies for building craftsmanship in work and thought.

Powerful Projects

It may sound obvious, but the first step in encouraging high-quality student work is to have assignments that inspire and challenge students. There's only so much care and creativity that a student can put into filling in the blanks on a commercially produced worksheet.

I've seen many thoughtful and effective assignment models in the schools I've visited. In my own building, we structure most student assignments within projects. We have a thematic curriculum: teachers use multidisciplinary themes (architecture, amphibians, ancient Greece, and so on) for weeks or months at a time, and within these themes students complete projects. These projects are the primary framework through which skills and understandings are learned. They are not extensions of the curriculum or extras when the required work is done. They are themselves at the core of the curriculum. In the course of a thematic study there may be three or four significant projects, most of which require research, writing skills, drafting skills, and sometimes mathematical or scientific skills. In the course of these projects there are usually traditional skill lessons and traditional informational lectures as in any school. The difference is that these skills are put to immediate use in the service of an original project with high student investment.

When I share beautiful student work from my classroom with others, I'm often asked how the students came to be this way, how they came to care so much about doing quality work. This is what I say: Most of my students have been doing this since they were four years old. They entered a school culture where high-quality projects are celebrated everywhere in the building. They didn't spend their years reading textbooks in unison or filling in blanks on worksheets—since pre-school and Kindergarten they've been creating books, drafting maps, researching local history, designing experiments. By the time I get them as fifth and sixth graders the ethic is there, the understanding is there, the motivation is there.

When I travel around the country to work with public schools I often bring a precious cargo home with me: memories of student projects presented to me by teachers or by the students themselves, and if I'm especially lucky, evidence or copies of great student projects themselves.

First graders in Mendocino, California, as part of a study of birds, decided to create an informative website about birds for children their age. They did lots of research but found that much of the material available was too difficult for young students and could not find answers to many of their questions. They went to their classroom computer, got online, and put out a request for expert help at sites for birders. They were overwhelmed with replies, and ended up hearing from experts all over the country who answered their questions personally, via email, and gave them regional updates on birds. With adult help the students used a web-authoring program and built their site using the wealth of information they had gathered.

First graders in Peter Thulson's class at the Rocky Mountain School of Expeditionary Learning in Denver were studying camping. They wanted to create a guide to camping for little kids. Some of them were scared at the idea of camping and many didn't know too much about it. They read about camping trips and interviewed people about camping trips. They worked for weeks on drafts of explanations and illustrations. Then they put their rough draft camping guide to the real test. They went camping together overnight as a whole class and followed it. Not surprisingly, they found they needed lots of revisions! Back in the classroom, their guide was redone with more wisdom.

Fourth graders working with teacher Steven Levy in Lexington, Massachusetts, not only designed and built their own desks with hand tools and pegs but also, in order to raise money for the project, grew and harvested wheat, built machines to separate and grind the wheat berries, ground flour, baked bread, sold the bread, started a non-profit company to finance their project with community business investors buying shares. With the capital they raised, they bought lumber for the job. Steven chronicles this remarkable project in his book *Starting from Scratch*.

Fourth graders in David Cornwell's class in Denver, in a study of Henry David Thoreau, built a full-scale replica of Thoreau's cabin on the school playground from the book *Walden*. They then raised money and, as a class, flew to Boston and visited Walden Pond and where they spent a week staying in a house by the pond. They visited the historic sites of Boston and, with Steven Levy's class in Lexington, reenacted the battle of Lexington on the town common: the scene of the shot heard 'round the world.

Sixth graders working with teachers Deb Fordice and Geri Maloy in Dubuque, Iowa, were involved with a local nursing home in a service project that paired students with seniors. They built a relationship over time through visits and interviews, and each student prepared a portrait and a full biography of his or her senior partner as a gift. The partnership program this project began received a $25,000 grant when the quality of the work and the relationships became public.

Middle school students at the Raphael Hernandez School in Boston took on a study of vacant lots in their Roxbury neighborhood. They researched the history of the sites, interviewed the neighborhood members regarding what uses they would prefer for the lots. They collaborated with officials from city hall and faculty and students from the Harvard School of Landscape Design. Eventually, they drafted blueprints and scale models of possible buildings, gardens, or playgrounds the sites might support. Their proposals were presented formally to the mayor of Boston and staff members from his office, and one of the sites was later converted to community gardens.

Not all projects are major endeavors or community service efforts, however. In my school, small projects that are good vehicles for teaching skills are done all the time. Yet, even these small projects are done with care and shared with a wider audience.

Projects don't generally have a great reputation in schooling. This poor reputation is often deserved. I need to explain that the project model we use is very different from the models of my youth. When I was a student in elementary school, doing projects meant getting ready for the annual science fair. This was the structure: My teacher would say, In one month we're having our Science Fair. Projects are due May 1. Good luck.

Here are some problems I have with the science fair model. The projects had nothing to do with what we were studying. Instead of being a culmination of our learning that could inspire dedication and quality in our daily work, the fair was like a visiting carnival, disconnected from school learning. Students, or their parents, made arbitrary topic choices, perhaps based on what materials were around the house or what a sibling had done already. We had no knowledge of what our peers were working on and therefore little interest in their final products. Since the projects were done entirely at home, often with parent help, students who came from homes privileged with money, time, or stability had an enormous advantage. As a child I could never tell how the teachers could discern how much of the project, if any, was actually done by the student.

We had no idea what good science was. We didn't understand validity or significance in data; we didn't understand control conditions and variables. We were never taught the stages of building and testing a hypothesis, nor how to break down a project into a sensible progression of steps. We didn't learn time management and so some of us—I was definitely in this category—ran around frantically the night before the fair trying to throw something together. People say that students learn from their mistakes when they face the consequences, but I didn't seem to: every year I ran around in the same last-minute panic.

On the day of the fair, most students brought in work but some had nothing at all: they were failures. Much of the work was last minute and some looked suspiciously like the work of an adult. Never having critiqued a science project or learned any of the qualities that would distinguish a good project, we students walked around clueless as to how to assess the work—and we focused only on what looked good. Later, ribbons magically appeared on certain projects, but this just confused and irritated us because they weren't the ones that we liked. The assessment criteria were a total mystery. When the fair ended there was little impact or carry-over in terms of understanding and quality in our daily work.

We did, actually, have a second project model: book projects. It was identical to the science fair protocol except that we were allowed to work with a partner. This is how it went for me in fourth grade: My teacher announced that team book projects were due in one month. My friend Doug asked me if I wanted to be his partner. I said yes. We forgot about it for about 28 days, then, with a reminder in class that the project was due that week, we got in gear.

I rode my bike over to Doug's house after school and we sat down to discuss the matter. Doug suggested we do our project on a book called *Pecos Bill*. I told him I hadn't read the book. He told me it didn't matter; we just needed a diorama of the old west. He described a scene from the book and I agreed to assemble it in my basement from a shoebox and some sand and my little brother's cowboy figures. I drew a nice backdrop. I took it to class on time, unlike some of our friends who failed, and we got an A on the project. I still have no idea who Pecos Bill was.

In contrast, the project model in the school where I teach is predicated on every child succeeding. Not just finishing, but producing work that represents excellence for that child. Though some of the work is done as homework, the *classroom is the hub of creation, the project workshop*. The *overall* quality of work that emerges from the workshop is a concern for every member in it. If *any* student is failing to succeed or producing work without care, it is a concern for *every* student. There is a sense of whole class pride in the quality of learning and products in the workshop, and there is a sense of peer pressure to keep up with the standard. These projects are made public and every student knows it. Anything weak reflects on all of us.

Projects have assessment rubrics, checklists, which make it clear just what is expected of each student. These rubrics spell out exactly what components are required in the project, what the time-line for completion is, and on what qualities and dimensions the project will be judged. Often these rubrics are constructed in collaboration with the students themselves.

Projects are structured to make it difficult for students to fall far behind or fail. They are broken down into clear components and students progress through checkpoints to insure they are keeping up. In my classroom, we often have large public checklists on the wall of all the components due for a certain project, and student monitors give updates at our morning meeting of who is caught up and who is falling behind. Through conferences and critique sessions with teachers and peers student progress is assessed and sustained throughout the creation process.

Because students work at different paces and levels, projects have built-in flexibility to allow for the range of abilities. Most projects have mandatory components completed by everyone in the class and optional components completed by those ahead of the pace. Though I have students whose reading levels vary by ten years on standardized assessments—students reading at an adult level and students with severe learning disabilities—all of these students complete the mandatory components of projects to their highest degree of capability and sophistication.

Though the process is universal the products are not uniform. If every student is preparing a design model for a municipal building, much of the skill and knowledge required is common to all: understanding community needs, design principles, zones of use, code issues, building an architectural program, layout conventions, measurement and geometry, drafting to scale, use of architectural tools, model building techniques. The process involves contacting architects and municipal officials, protocols for contacting adults politely, conducting a phone and email interview, note-taking, writing business and thank-you letters, arranging for visits to sites, taking on-site photographs, or doing sketches. Within this frame however there is latitude for personal choice and artistry: choosing the type of building, deciding whom to contact, gathering information, arranging contacts and interviews, and putting together a design that is wholly original and yet addresses all the requirements and constraints of real life.

Even in Kindergarten, where the climate is less high-pressure, the projects are original and carefully guided to ensure each student grows and is successful. Last year my students helped their Kindergarten buddies present a completed project at a school-wide assembly. The Kindergartners had picked apples, carved a face in the apple (with help from their older buddies), soaked the apples in salt water, and let them age and shrink to create old, human-like faces. They built an apple person around their carved head, created clothing, a background diorama, and created their life: name, age, family, and other vital statistics. They wrote a story about their character, designed a home for their character, and described their character's life. The Kindergartners' skills ranged widely in reading, writing, and fine motor work, but each succeeded, with support, in building a beautifully crafted final product, with all the originality and zany quality that is the hall-mark of the five-year-old imagination.

Building Literacy Through the Work

After sharing powerful student project work with teachers and administrators I'm often met with this response: This work is amazing, but we don't actually have time to work on projects; we need to focus on basic skills and literacy. We need to teach kids how to read and write well before we can spend time on projects and thematic studies.

This shows me that my message was not clear. As much as I try to explain that the projects I'm describing are a context for teaching skills—basic skills and high order skills—the word *project* suggests to most people an extra activity after the real curriculum and instruction is done. I need to make explicit that we use these projects to teach children to be strong readers and writers and mathematicians. All of our thematic studies are rich in literature and informational text; almost every project includes substantial reading, writing, and research; many projects are centered on great authors or books. It's not simply that this work entails lots of reading and writing, but that we explicitly teach reading and writing skills formally during the work. Rather than limit the time available for addressing literacy skills, this approach builds in literacy instruction all day long.

Two of the projects that my students received some recognition for were the Radon Study and the Water Study, in which we assessed the safety of homes in town regarding levels of radon gas and purity of well water. Both of these are usually described as science studies or science projects and this is a fair description, since my students were working as scientists for months. What may not be so apparent is the amount of math embedded in the study—all students became facile with data analysis and graphing, and all became proficient users of the Microsoft Excel spreadsheet program. Even less apparent perhaps is the amount of time we focused on reading and writing skills.

To gain the necessary background for our work we were immersed for months in written resources. The information we needed was not found in elementary or secondary science textbooks; it was not presented in the shallow, predictable format common to textbooks. We read published scientific papers, newspaper articles, government reports, informational pamphlets, and selections from scientific books. We read professional scientific catalogues in order to order supplies and we read instructional booklets explaining test kits. There was not a piece of text we used that didn't require careful reading lessons to make sure we understood it well. I taught my students to be capable readers of science material and informational text in myriad contexts; the opportunities for genuine literacy instruction were continuous.

Together we made sense of challenging material, learned lots of new vocabulary, and importantly, learned to make sense of information presented in a wide variety of formats. The motivation was intense. We needed to understand this stuff to do important work; the whole town was counting on us and people's lives and health depended on our success. We took our reading lessons seriously.

In order to prepare written reports of the test results and the implications of those results—individual reports were sent to families and a collective report of the big picture was presented to the town—students needed to learn to write as scientists. We read scientific reports and analyzed their written formats and language. Writing lessons connected to this work were daily. We looked at data together and discussed as a group the most accurate, responsible, and ethical way to present those data in words to a family and to the town. We practiced describing the tests and results in written format, critiqued our work, and rewrote our descriptions. With people's lives and health at stake, taking care with the details of our language was vital. We could cause misunderstanding or even panic if we worded things poorly; we were meticulous in crafting our wording for every written product. Since every student in the class was responsible for writing individual family letters and reports, there was an ethic of precision in written language that was ubiquitous.

A visitor to the classroom during our thematic study of water who was looking for evidence of literacy instruction and learning might not have even thought to look at the science work. Our reading work during this water theme centered on books such as *Huckleberry Finn*, and included studies of Greek mythology and of Homer's *Odyssey*, much of which was read in a comparative study of five different children's versions and three adult translations. Our writing work included projects on *The Odyssey* and additionally, each student created an original novel that took place in a water environment. Our work in literary analysis and creative writing during this time was vibrant and important, but I can't say I think it was more important in developing literacy skills than the "science" work; all of this was important literacy work to me.

When people ask me when I have time to teach reading and

writing skills in the midst of this project culture, I think, All day. This is what I do all day.

Genuine Research

There is almost nothing more exciting in education than being engaged in genuine research—research where the teacher and students are exploring new ground together. When I visit schools or attend educational conferences where students and teachers have been working together to uncover local history or investigate environmental conditions, the energy is unparalleled. Kids and teachers both can't wait to talk with me, to explain their ideas, their problems, their hypotheses, their results. The students are bubbling over with stories and new knowledge. When I was a student myself I never really got a taste for this passion.

I spent years doing science experiments. We called them experiments, but we didn't really experiment. These were scientific procedures, prescribed by a book, that we were instructed to follow so that we could achieve the prescribed result, a result that our teacher knew ahead of time. Following the procedure competently and efficiently, and reaching the intended end point was the goal of this work. (In fact, students who decided to really experiment with the materials generally got into trouble.) These procedures could, with good teaching, be useful hands-on demonstrations of concepts or principles. But the excitement of real discovery was never there.

Often I engaged in written research: looking up prescribed topics in the encyclopedia as I was instructed and paraphrasing what was written there as a report. This process taught us skills and was governed by standards, and one would imagine held real opportunities for quality. Unfortunately, the directions and time constraints made strategies for truly excellent research—a broad search for sources, a deep analysis of data, developing original hypotheses, making discoveries, and preparing a final report crafted through many drafts—not particularly feasible. Of course, we didn't even *have* this vision of excellence in research; we just worked to do an efficient job of putting the organization and phrasing of the encyclopedia into our own paragraphs and words.

As an adult, a teacher, I realize that the opportunities for genuine research are everywhere. Every town or city is full of public records that sit neglected, environmental conditions that no one is monitoring, businesses and families whose histories have never been explored. Every community is full of senior citizens, immigrants, craftspeople, veterans, and survivors of all kinds whose stories have never been told.

When Kathy Greeley's students at The Graham and Parks Middle School in Cambridge, Massachusetts, prepared a guidebook to their city community, each student researched a building through public records and interviews of community members. When students at King Middle School in Portland, Maine, prepared a field guide to the wildlife in the bay near their school, they did research in books and on computers and also put on wet suits, masks, snorkels, and flippers and went into the bay for real-life observation and sketching.

No child is too young to be offered this opportunity. While some unfortunate Kindergartners are required to spend their days filling in worksheets, there is probably no period of life better attuned to investigation and discovery than as a five-year-old. Some of my most exciting research has been with young children. When I was working with first graders many years ago we took on a study of land snails. Each student had his or her own snail to care for; pairs of students shared a small terrarium. We learned more about snails than almost anyone on earth would want to know. Our research had a single goal: to keep the snails healthy and happy. We needed to know what foods and conditions they preferred. We began by looking at existing resources, but my students were quickly disappointed in the knowledge that was out there already. The list of what snails would eat was short and gave no idea as to their preferences. After learning the types of foods that would be safe to feed snails, my students began testing just about every brand of bread, cereal, cookie, vegetable, and fruit they could find, and compiling lists of how quickly and completely things were eaten. We ended up with a chart of over 140 preferred foods, with annotations on many.

Students designed experiments to determine what living conditions worked best. Did snails prefer heat or cold, light or dark, black or white, moist or dry, yellow or red? Using construction paper, light bulbs, ice cubes, sandpaper, glass, wood, fabric, soil types, moss, plants, perfumes, and all sorts of materials, students built experimental environments. The first time the students put a snail on the line between red and black paper the snail turned and moved onto the red. Some students decided the snail preferred red but we discussed as a group the danger of such an assumption. At the suggestion of the group, we tried the experiment ten times and most times the snail turned toward the red. Some were convinced that red was preferred but others remembered our discussions of variables. There are other variables, they pointed out. The red paper was closer to the window, the light. Perhaps it was the light that attracted them. The black paper was smoother; perhaps it was texture. Maybe the snail couldn't see color at all but preferred light shades over dark shades. So we tried the experiment again and again, trying to limit the variables to see if we could determine whether our result meant something. These students not only learned about snails, but also learned experimental technique.

Opportunities for original statistical research in education are almost endless. My students have joined data analysis to service in a wide variety of projects. In addition to water and radon testing, my students have prepared demographic analyses of changes in town population as a service to the town government. They have surveyed and analyzed school climate and safety as a service to the school committee. They have analyzed data sets of international financial conditions to help focus our charitable contributions.

Teaching how to do original research doesn't come easily to many teachers. Some teachers explain to me: If it's not in the science or social studies textbook, or in the new state curriculum frameworks, I'm not allowed to mention it, or just as common, We're only given 30 minutes for science, three days a week—these are district rules. To teachers working under such constraints I give this advice: Align the research with a mandated curriculum topic and then stretch the time and travel restriction rules as much as you can.

The bigger issue is teacher confidence and experience. Many teachers have never had the opportunity to engage in original research themselves and they're afraid to try. In science particularly, elementary school teachers frequently tell me that they have little background or understanding of real research. My first suggestion to such teachers is to let go of their expectation that they need to be the expert in everything, the person who knows all the answers. If they see themselves instead as the lead researcher, a co-investigator working along with their students, they can learn along with their students. Teachers need to model standards for scientific and historical technique, but they can find true experts—scientists and historians—to help them and the students.

In my school, teachers meet with outside experts during the planning stages of investigations, bring the experts into the classroom to help guide and critique the work, and take the students to meet with them at their office or lab or at a fieldwork site. My students often contact experts through email, letters, and phone calls during the course of a study.

We treat our experts royally. We honor them with respect, courtesy, genuine interest in their field. As teachers, we prepare the students not only to be polite to the experts, but also to appreciate their expertise, understand their individual work, and use it well. Students greet them in the parking lot, carry their supplies to the classroom, serve them food and drink, help them set up, and of course follow up with thank you's and copies of our work. Many local experts in my area have become life-long friends and supporters of the school.

The Power of the Arts

A few years ago I hosted visitors to my school who went with students on a long tour visiting classrooms from the pre-school up through the sixth grade. When they returned they seemed confused. They were science teachers and having seen a videotape of a water study we had done they assumed this was a science magnet school. Now, after the tour, they said: This looks like an arts magnet school. The Kindergartners were painting large wood sculptures they had built; the fourth graders were developing photographs they had taken and were working on the computer to edit digital photographs; a sixth-grade girl was giving a cello recital in a classroom as part of a reading project; the hallways were covered with murals, drawings, paintings, blueprints, and collages.

Many people in education debate whether studying music helps math test scores, or whether visual arts instruction raises spatial intelligence in ways that the SAT will measure. People who feel that test scores should determine the extent to which arts should be a part of the curriculum need to put down their research for a moment and visit a school in which arts are taken seriously. They need to listen to the Harlem Boys Choir or watch the Dance Theater of Harlem youth performances. The passion, the commitment, the discipline arts can engender in children is not in question when you see it in action.

Steve Seidel, director of the Harvard Project Zero research team, talks of the draw toward beauty that students have, that communities have, that all humans have. The appeal of the aesthetic. He points out that this has been a powerful driving force behind the accomplishments of cultures through history. Why are we using this force so rarely in our schools to light a fire in the hearts of children?

The question for me is not whether we can afford to keep arts in our schools but how we can ensure that students put artistic care into everything that they do. In all schools, almost all original work is shared with others through some artistic medium. It might be expository writing, fiction, poetry; displays, diagrams, maps, illustrations, posters, models; computer presentations, photographs, slides, video; drama, music, or movement. Every written or graphic presentation of work, every oral presentation or performance can be, and should be, prepared with aesthetic consideration, critiqued and refined aesthetically, and viewed with aesthetic eyes. When students learn to love art, to do art well—whether it's drama, music, calligraphy, photography—they learn to present themselves and their work with care.

My graduate school friend Eiko was preparing resumes to send to prospective employers in this country and in her native Japan. For U.S. employers, her resume was done on a computer; for Japanese employers, done by hand with a calligraphic pen. I would never word process my resume for Japanese eyes, she told me; they judge my character, in part, by my calligraphy. Here's a culture with an aesthetic vision that makes sense to me: everything is viewed aesthetically. The arrangement of food on a plate, the way one is greeted in a doorway, the layout of a home. Art is everything and everything is art. When this ethic becomes part of a classroom, each student report, display, thank-you card, and math graph becomes an opportunity to present something well.

Art in my school is not something that happens on Tuesday afternoons from 1:45 to 2:20, but a part of everything that we do. Artists are brought in to share, to inspire, to critique—authors, musicians, sculptors, dancers, actors—and to teach the skills of their discipline. When sixth-grade students share their portfolios of work to the graduation panel, there are often live performances of instrumental or vocal music and videotaped performances of drama and dance, and the displays of their academic work are infused with artistic products.

We even take our materials seriously. My students use professional-quality materials in the classroom and they know it. When we visit artists, architects, or scientists, the students immediately begin a discussion about tools and materials. In the same way that students obsess about getting the best sneakers, mountain bikes, or video game systems, my students obsess about getting the best erasers, colored pencils, calligraphy pens, brushes, templates. There is good reason for this. When students spend weeks drafting blueprints it makes a difference that the white eraser they use doesn't abrade and tear their paper and that their colored pencils are soft, rich, and lay down vibrant color.

Clearly good-quality science and art supplies are expensive, and it takes a commitment to finding or raising money for them and building a climate in which materials are treated as precious. My students know exactly the cost of all of our materials, and know exactly how angry the class and I will be if they're lost or misused. I stock my classroom with good supplies so that any student from any financial background has access to what he or she needs. I also, though, encourage students to buy their own, because once they own their own supplies they value them, learn to label them, care for them, and can take them home at the year's end. My teaching team sends a letter to every family with a detailed list of supplies that would be useful, and suggests to parents that perhaps as a birthday or holiday gift, some of these supplies would make a fine alternative to a CD or video game cartridge. Many families of limited means have found a way to equip their child with a fine calligraphy pen or a colored pencil set, and I assure you those children were proud. When I talk with former students who've finished high school or college, they'll often mention that they still have their Berol Prismacolor colored pencil set from sixth grade, and still use it.

I visited a large, troubled urban middle school on a consultation and observed classes. After school the teachers complained that their students just didn't care. My observations during the day were almost the opposite: most students cared deeply and were almost obsessed—with art. They listened to music every chance they had; they carried Walkmans everywhere, trying to sneak in a song at every possible moment. They memorized lyrics, critiqued lyrics, wrote them down in their notebooks, and sang them in the hallways. They drew pictures during class whenever the teacher wasn't looking; they wrote their names in different lettering styles. When they spoke with me about their lives they were anything but disaffected: they were passionate, idealistic, angry, and confused. Art helped them make sense of their turmoil. Unfortunately, arts were no longer a part of the school curriculum—a victim of budget cuts and new priorities. The idea that some of this artistic passion could be harnessed and infused into a commitment to school was not being discussed. There was no school chorus, no school musical, no school mural to draw these students in and engage them to work together. There was no project work with artistic dimensions in which students could learn discipline and control of a medium, in which they could learn to express themselves and grapple with their identity issues in the service of creating something of value.

I visited an elite private school known for its arts program and walked into a painting studio. The ceilings were high and had skylights. The walls were covered with striking canvases done by students. Classical music from a paint-splattered tape player on a messy counter filled the room. The teacher sat by a student who worked at an easel, critiquing a rich, Impressionistic painting that the student was creating. Five other students were transfixed in front of easels; they didn't even notice my entrance. This was the entire class: six third-grade students. I felt inspired and sad at the same time. Every student deserves this, I thought.

Models

When I was an apprentice builder the master carpenter who taught me my craft rarely wasted time with long explanations. When he wanted to teach me the proper framing for a door or what a good miter joint looked like in window trim, he showed me an example. No amount of words could convey what one good model taught me. I carried around that vision in my head and I always knew what I was a striving for: I had a picture of what quality work looked like.

I want my students to carry around pictures in their head of quality work. It's not enough to make a list, a rubric, of what makes a good essay or a good science experiment. This is an important step, but it doesn't leave a picture, a vision, an inspiration. It's not even enough to read a great piece of literature together and analyze the writing, or to look at the work of a great scientist. If I want my students specifically to write a strong essay, to design a strong experiment, I need to show them what a great essay or experiment looks like. We need to admire models, find inspiration in them, and analyze their strengths and weaknesses. We need to figure out together what it is that makes this work strong.

And so I spend my life collecting good work. Most of it comes from my own students, but I gather work from other classrooms in my school and from schools I visit. When I begin a new project with my students, I go to my library of models and pin-up work, show slides of work, photocopies of work, and together we marvel and admire, we critique and analyze. My students are excited to see models of everything. Whatever we're undertaking, whether it's a math challenge or dance performance or a science investigation, my students cry out for models to set the standard of what they're aiming for, and to give them a vision of their goal. The models stay on display on the walls or on the counters so that students can return again and again to weigh their efforts against strong work from the past. I save models of the final products, and also models of the many earlier drafts of work so that students can see the creation and refinement process.

Many years ago, while attending meetings of a teacher/portfolio group, I noticed that teachers often shared perceptive self-evaluations and self-assessments written by their students. This seemed valuable. I wanted to try it. I did try it, but without success. I prepared forms that asked students to reflect on their strengths, weaknesses, and growth. I prepared reflective forms on particular projects and general forms for them to use to assess their growth as students. I generally got one word and one-sentence answers; the critique tended to be shallow and focused on neatness or written mechanics. There was little real depth or insight.

I returned to my teacher group, raised my hand, and confessed my utter failure. My friend Kathy Greeley laughed at me. Aren't you the king of models?, she asked. Don't you always say you need models for everything? Why didn't you show them models of good reflection? I felt pretty dumb. I realized I didn't even *have* any such models. So I borrowed a model—a beautiful self-reflection by an eighth-grade English student in the class of my friend Kathy Howard. I took that model back to class and together we read it and analyzed it.

I challenged my students: Could you write something like this? Do you understand yourselves and your work at this level? No way, they said, she's in eighth grade. No wonder she writes so well. We looked at the piece closely; we spent most of an hour looking at the vocabulary, the ideas, the tone, the humor, and the honesty. Then I sent them home to try for themselves. For the first time I got reflective work that was powerful and perceptive. Was it derivative and imitative of the model piece? Absolutely. But it was also personal and honest. Some of it was terrific. I haven't had to use that original eighth-grader's model again—I now have piles of sixth-grade models that shine.

I've been criticized at times by educators for using models so much. All of the work will be copies, they say; the models will stifle the creativity and originality of everyone's work. There is validity in their concern: my students borrow ideas from the models and from each other all the time. But I don't mind at all. In fact, I encourage imitation as a place to begin. As a student, I learned to write by copying the styles of great authors; I learned to paint by copying the styles of great painters. This is one way to learn, an excellent way to learn, in fact. Does it matter that my students sometimes use former or current students as their models instead of using famous masters?

I encourage this practice so regularly that I explicitly describe and present what I call *tribute work*. Tribute work is the work of a student who built off of, borrowed ideas from, or imitated the work of a particular former or current student. This practice is not called copying or cheating in my classroom; it's acknowledged as legitimate and wise practice. Recently a former student, now an adult, visited my classroom and I introduced her to the class. One sixth-grade boy was startled. You're Jennifer?, he asked. Not the Jennifer who created the blueprints for the cylindrical house and barn? He couldn't believe it. He approached her. I worked for months on blueprints for a cylindrical house inspired by your design, he said. I can't believe I'm actually meeting you! I didn't really think of you as being real! He walked to his portfolio and showed her his work—a beautiful set of blueprints and an original design—clearly inspired by Jennifer's work. They sat down together to look at his work, absolutely a tribute to her work from long ago. This is an honor to meet you, he said.

I try to keep a wide range of models for any given project so that students don't think there is a single correct response to an assignment. When beginning character portraits, I present a slide show of dozens of portraits done by previous students and we critique and analyze each one. I keep models that are tributes to earlier models and we discuss their similar and original qualities.

The search for models makes every day exciting. I never know when a stunning drawing, an elegant poem, or a brilliant math solution is going to appear. When they arrive they are gifts of incredible value. I have some models I've used for twenty years and they still inspire. I beg, bargain, and plead with students to loan me their work as models. I make both black and white and color photocopies of work, I photograph work, I take slides of work, I scan work, and I videotape work. Last week I ran into a former student at the supermarket, pushing a cart full of groceries and her young daughter. She smiled and asked a question: Still have a copy of my blueprints?

Like all teachers, I search for models outside of the classroom: in literature, in the academic world, in the professional world, in life. Student-generated models have a particular value, and models from the real world have their own particular value. When students look at the work of a professional writer, engineer, architect, illustrator, or athlete, they see the standards of real life and gain the grand vision of where this can lead.

Perhaps the most important models of all are people. In my school, and in many schools, we try to bring in inspirational experts in all fields to share with students their knowledge and, just as important, their passion for their studies, their craft, their profession. Similarly, my hope as a teacher is to always be a model of excitement in learning, to have students see the genuine confusion, frustration, and joy I experience when we discover things together and build good work together. I want to be a model of courtesy, dedication, hard work, and fairness. When a guest enters our classroom, students watch the efforts I put into being a gracious host: this is a model. When our guest leaves, I sit down with students and struggle to craft a beautiful thank-you card just as they do: this is a model.

My favorite models are the students themselves. When one of my students or a younger student in the school does something extraordinary—an artistic presentation, an intellectual achievement, an act of courage or kindness—we stop and appreciate. We discuss it, remember it, and hold it in our minds and hearts as an image. Two years ago a disabled younger student did a dance performance in front of the whole school. My students talked about it all year. Whenever one of them was trying to marshal the bravery to take a risk, someone would bring up that image, that child, that model of courage.

Multiple Drafts

When I was a student in public school I turned in final draft work every hour, every day. Work was generally done in one draft, and we kept cranking it out and passing it in. Even if we cared about quality there wasn't much we could do: we needed to get things done and passed in.

One of the first things a school or classroom can do to improve the quality of student work is to get off this treadmill. This doesn't mean an end to deadlines—the real world is full of deadlines—but rather a clear distinction between rough research, rough drafts, and finished, polished final draft work. It means final drafts may take days or weeks to complete. It means a different type of pressure: not just pressure to turn in enough work but pressure to produce something of real value.

It took me a year to design my home. I wasn't working in a CAD program; my drafting was done by hand. I was up late at night for months, crouched over a drafting table with pencils, scales, templates, and white erasers. Every few weeks I'd complete a draft and review it with my wife, who would then suggest changes. I'd go over it with my builder friends and they'd suggest changes. Then I'd go back to the drafting board and begin again. When I'd been through six or seven drafts, things looked like they might be settling in to a final design. I bought some foam-core board and began a scale model. This was getting exciting.

My wife took one look at the model and shook her head. That's what you're thinking? That's what it will be like? She wasn't pleased at all. I pointed out that she had looked at the blueprints for months and approved them. Well, she said, I didn't know it would be like *that*.

I went back to the drafting board. Even after all the sensible advice from friends and family, some things I refused to change. I'd spent many years building fairly standard homes for others and I knew I wanted this house to be unique. The core of the house was an enormous stone fireplace—I would gather the local stone—and the stone chimney was so wide that it had an archway cut out of its center. The stairs, beefy custom treads, slabs of local maple, wrapped around behind the chimney so that you could look down through the archway into a greenhouse when walking upstairs. At the stair landing there was a window seat that was big enough for sleeping and a storage shelf and secret compartment underneath. When I budgeted for the chimney, the oak beams, the maple floors and trim, the many windows facing the hills to make this home a bright, passive solar one, I was far beyond our modest budget even if I built it myself. I kept the important features, took my wife's good advice on changes, and shrunk the house down. It was now just a two bedroom, one bathroom house. But a very cool one. With the kids grown and moved out, it was enough house for us.

Many months and quite a few drafts later both the plans and the model received family and building inspector approval. We broke ground in April and began framing. I tried to follow my plans but of course, now that it was real scale, they weren't quite right. My wife would suggest changes, my building partners would suggest changes, even I would look at interior wall placements or door placements and see that an adjustment would help. I ran into problems and consulted other builders and factory representatives—made more changes. Standing on the second floor deck, looking out on the mountains, my brother visiting from California pointed out that the bathroom window wouldn't give the best view from the toilet. I didn't want to move the window—it was aligned with a lower window in the exterior elevation—but the house wasn't plumbed yet so we moved the toilet.

I tell people I designed my house. When my house appeared in *Fine Homebuilding* magazine, I was listed as the designer/builder, and I was proud. The truth is this: If my house had a list of credits like those that appear at the end of a movie, it would be a long list. At this point I can't even remember which ideas were mine and which came from my son, my electrician, my building partners.

I tell my students the story of my house every year. I show them my blueprints, share all the problems and changes. I explain that, like many home designs, it went through more than ten drafts. They critique my early ideas, my finished plans, and I take them to my home and they critique the real thing. When they get discouraged on a project, five drafts completed and still not a final in sight, they take heart in my story. At least it won't take me a *year*, they say, like you took on your blueprints.

When I was a student in elementary school, needing to do a second draft of a piece of work meant one thing: You blew it. You failed. If I turned in an assignment that the teacher didn't accept, it felt pretty serious. She accepted almost everything. The norm was one draft; anything else was a failure. Any student who got his or her work back for a second draft was ashamed, whether they showed it outwardly or not. This is still the case in most schools today: a piece of work that is not ready in one draft carries the stigma of weakness or failure.

In my school and in many school's I've visited, teachers struggle to build a different ethic. What could you possibly achieve of quality in a single draft? Would you ever put on a play without rehearsals? Give a concert without practicing first? How much editing went into every book that we read? Students in my classroom often take pride in their dedication to drafts: I did *thirteen* drafts of this cover, they brag.

Students need to know from the outset that quality means rethinking, reworking, and polishing. They need to feel that they will be celebrated, not ridiculed, for going back to the drawing board. When I have students draft blueprints for houses, they know that the *minimum* number of drafts is four. Every student must have at least one rough sketch on regular paper, one expanded draft on large art paper, one scale drawing on large graph paper, and a final draft on professional vellum. Most students go through six to ten drafts, but nobody, nobody does a single draft house design— not in real life, not in the classroom.

Teachers point out to me that preparing numerous drafts would be too discouraging for young students. I reply that when I taught Kindergarten and first grade I did much the same thing as I do now. I would tell students we were going to do four different *versions* of a drawing of a house. Each day I would teach a new lesson about drawing, and they would do a new version. On Friday they would each get to pick their favorite version, and we would have a discussion about which versions they liked best. They soon began complaining if I didn't allow them to do more than one version of a piece of work.

Guests ask me how we ever get work done in the classroom. With so many drafts being prepared and some students doing four and some doing ten, how do you ever keep track of what's going on, and how do you ever get every student to finish his or her work? I have no magic answer. How does it work in real life? We have a deadline, just like in life. Our exhibition is in three weeks. The Board of Health is meeting on Tuesday. The author of the book on

Shutesbury history is meeting with the printer on May 15. We have checklist charts in student portfolios and a poster-sized checklist on the wall. We are working to deadline and there's pressure. I push students hard and they push each other hard. This is what life is like. Do I worry about students falling behind or rushing ahead? All the time. Every day.

At the end of each year my students present their work to a panel of educators and community members as a requirement for graduation. Each student sits alone in front of the panel—administrators, teachers, school committee members, town officials—and presents her or his achievements and challenges. For twelve years every student has done this presentation and has done it well, be they students with physical and behavioral challenges, students with emotional and cognitive problems, students who are confident, or students who are terrified. The fact that they have all succeeded is not just luck. We don't do this in one draft.

In the first week of school I show videotapes of former students presenting to the panel and I remind students that at the end of the year it will be they who are presenting. They have models in their mind. They spend the entire year building a strong portfolio and practicing presenting it. They present projects to their classmates, to their parents, to the school as a whole, and to classroom guests. They get feedback and critique all year long. Two weeks before the presentations we again view videotapes and put those models in our minds. We look over rubrics of what constitutes a strong presentation. We review portfolios and begin selecting projects. We put together presentation display boards and each student has a partner to support and critique through rehearsal. Students rehearse in front of peers, family, teachers, and sometimes in front of the video camera. We view rehearsals on video so students can watch themselves and learn. By the time each student walks into that conference room, their work in hand

and their partner beside them as an assistant, they are on draft ten, or maybe draft twenty.

Critique

Teachers give critique to individual students via their verbal comments during the school day and through their written comments on student work. Many teachers also pair off students and ask them to critique each other's writing. I suggest teachers take critique to a whole new level and make critique a habit of mind that suffuses the classroom in all subjects. Formal critique sessions are a cornerstone of my classroom practice, and the informal culture of critique they spawn is at the core of work improvement.

Critique in most classroom settings has a singular audience and a limited impact: whether from a teacher or peer, it is for the edification of the author; the goal is to improve that particular piece. The formal critique in my classroom has a broader goal. I use whole-class critique sessions as a primary context for sharing knowledge and skills with the group. Sessions are structured to help students learn what constitutes good writing, math, science, or historical inquiry. We critique an individual piece of work, or a number of pieces, in a guided session together. What better way is there to teach the elements of a good essay or science experiment than to thoughtfully analyze together student-created models?

In my consulting work with schools, some of the most valuable contributions have been through opportunities to share this broader and deeper approach to critique. Sometimes I lead school faculties in critique sessions of student work; other times I lead demonstration critique sessions with a class of students as teachers observe. In both cases I strive to build excitement for, and understanding of, the incredible learning potential in looking carefully at student work together as a group.

I run critique sessions in my classroom every week, during some studies every day, or even more than once in a day. When teachers ask me when I could possibly find the time to fit in critique with all the lessons I need to teach, I explain that these critique sessions *are* the lessons. Rather than talk in the abstract about how to write well, how to compile a good bibliography, or how to prepare a data analysis, we sit as a group and critique examples of our attempts at this work, refining our criteria and vision of what constitutes excellence.

There are a number of formal critique protocols that I've learned from over the years. I've had the good fortune to work with Steve Seidel, an author of the Collaborative Assessment Protocol, and Joe MacDonald, an author of The Tuning Protocol. Both of these critique structures have been inspirations to me. In my own classroom, I use a protocol that is not nearly as elegant and complex as Steve's or Joe's; mine is designed as a quick and easy tool that I can use for thirty minutes in a pre-planned session or just as easily grab for a spontaneous five-minute session when I see the need.

I have just three rules.

Be Kind. It's essential that the critique environment feel safe, and the class and I are vigilant to guard against any hurtful comments. This includes sarcasm.

Be Specific. No comments such as *It's good* or *I like it*; these just waste our time.

Be Helpful. The goal is to help the individual and the class, not for the critic to be heard. Echoing the thoughts of others or cleverly pointing out details that are not significant to improving the work also wastes our time.

I also have guidelines that we try to use. In the heat of a good critique, we may abandon some of the guidelines, though we never abandon the rules.

The guidelines are these:

We try to begin with the author/designer of the work explaining her ideas and goals, and explaining what particular aspects of the work she is seeking help with.

We critique the work, not the person.

We try to begin our critique comments with something positive about the work, and then move on to constructive criticism.

We try to use *I statements* when possible: "I'm confused by this," rather than "This makes no sense."

We try to use a question format when possible: "I'm curious why you chose to begin with this . . . ?" or "Have you considered including . . . ?"

I use two distinct formal critique formats in my classroom.

In a *Gallery Critique,* the work of every child is displayed on boards or photocopied to read. We first look at all of the work silently before giving comments, and the focus is primarily positive: Students select examples from the gallery that impress them and we discuss why. Advantages to this format include creating positive pressure for every child to complete a draft of his or her work, generating ideas and models of strong work, and setting the tone for a whole-class standard of quality.

When doing an *In-Depth Critique,* we look at the work of a single student or group and spend a good deal of time critiquing it thoroughly. Advantages to this style include opportunities for teaching the vocabulary and concepts of the discipline from which the work emerges, for teaching what comprises good work in that discipline, and opportunities for modeling the detailed process of making the work stronger.

There are some specific logistical suggestions I give to staffs with whom I'm consulting regarding critiquing written work. I think that the typical strategy of pairing off kids to critique one another is not often particularly useful unless it's preceded by a formal class critique that gets students focused and excited about a specific dimension of writing. Also, try to differentiate between critiquing for specific content qualities and critiquing for mechanics (conventions); if this isn't clear, critique can quickly become just copyediting. When we do whole-class critique, we make sure that each student has a photocopy in hand or can see an overhead projection. We want our critique to focus closely on the written text, the specific language and structure, rather than on general impressions of its comment. In a gallery critique of writing we may look just at the first paragraph or first sentence of every student's work. Our critique is largely a search for good strategies and ideas that we can learn and borrow.

It's crucial to focus on vocabulary building in the critique process. To use a metaphor I learned, if we picture our critique as surgically dissecting a piece of work to improve it, our vocabulary is our kit of surgical tools. If we only have words like "it's good" or "it's bad," we are trying to do surgery with a meat cleaver. If we want to dissect the work carefully and put it back together well, we need a kit of precise tools. I teach the vocabulary of each discipline, and when we have guest critiques from outside experts, we make a list of all the new vocabulary tools we're given.

The vocabulary of a discipline is more than just its words: Each word represents a concept that can be hard to grasp until you have a word for it. In gallery critiques, students very often point out work in gallery critiques that they are drawn to, but they can't articulate just what it is that they like in the work—they just know they like it. Once they learn the vocabulary that describes the dimensions of the work they are often clear about exactly what impresses them.

The power of vocabulary to represent concepts was never more evident to me than in a critique visit we hosted years ago of the University of Massachusetts women's soccer team. I was coaching my students who formed a coed classroom soccer team and I thought to invite the UMass team, a nationally ranked squad, to visit us and help teach. Rather than have the visit be just an auto-graph session, I asked the UMass players to play a soccer game with us and then to critique our play. When they began their critique they immediately started using words that were unfamiliar to my students, words that described strategies or alignments on the field. My students not only learned the words but also learned to look at the field and at their movements entirely differently. The very next day my students' level of play took an enormous leap: I could hear them shouting out their new words as they moved up field in entire-ly new ways.

We use guest critique quite a bit. In our classroom studies of architecture over the years, we have depended on the kindness and expertise of local architects as our experts. Having professionals come into the classroom to critique student work is an exciting experience, quite different from the traditional model of inviting an expert simply to be a guest speaker. One year we had a different guest architect visit every Friday for a formal gallery critique. All week students obsessed over their work, hoping that their blueprint would be one of the ones chosen by our guest professional for com-ments. The motivation was intense. On Friday, all the work was posted on portable display boards and a professional architect would walk back and forth in front of the class, scrutinizing the work, and suddenly stop and point, Whose work is this? Who had this interesting idea? The proud student would raise his hand, ready to discuss his work.

We wrote down the professional vocabulary we learned at each critique and discussed the ideas and concepts we learned from the expert's comments.

A few years back, some researchers at Harvard Project Zero had grown skeptical that young students were capable of mature cri-tique; they were having trouble getting good examples in a middle school research setting. When I told them my fifth and sixth graders were engaged in what I believed was mature critique they looked doubtful. They asked if they could come visit with a video camera. I told my students that the Harvard folks weren't sure that kids as young as they were capable of real critique. This got their competitive spirit going: they couldn't wait for the video camera. Bring them on! they said.

It so happened that this group of students had watched a number of guest architects critique their work. They not only understood the issues involved in architectural critique but knew the language, the gestures, and the mannerisms of real architects. The researchers arrived and the video camera was set up. A student rose and paced back and forth stroking his chin. Jenny, he said to a student whose building design was posted, I *love* your concept. I see some issues with *practicality* though. You may need to rethink the flow of this entryway. The student then paused to smile at the camera. I don't know if the tape was useful due to all the hamming, but the critique of all the students was genuinely good.

Being the only teacher in the classroom, there is no way I can find the time to edit every line of writing in every draft and critique every idea. I need to build a class full of editors, architects, scientists, writers, and mathematicians who don't hesitate to continually critique each other's work. We have formal critique sessions regularly, but an important reason for this formal work is to hone the ability of the class members to critique each other informally. The bulk of our critique goes on all day long as students review each other's work again and again, asking for help, giving suggestions. When I sit at my desk and watch students working at tables, they pause regularly in their work to ask help from neighbors: How does this look to you? How does this sound? What do you think of this idea? My elementary students become so accustomed to the privilege of critique that after they have moved on to middle school or high school, they often drop by after school to ask if they can get some critique on a piece of work they are doing.

Making Work Public

Early in my building career I was asked to build a large outdoor staircase at a warehouse loading dock. I was nervous because I had an audience. The guys who worked in the warehouse—giant, over-weight guys riding forklifts—watched me work and shook their heads skeptically. They thought I was a joke—too young and too small to be taken seriously—and they made fun of me while wait-ing for new truckloads to arrive. When I finished the staircase it looked good but they were afraid to walk on it. They tried it out carefully, then with some confidence. Finally they all went out and jumped on it and smiled. From that day on I was known on the site as The Skinny Kid Who Built the Stairs. They treated me pretty well after this. As a carpenter I had strong incentive to care about the quality of my work: it was important and it was public.

I had no audience while doing my work when I was a student and no sense that my work meant something to someone. Actually, I did have a singular audience: my teacher. I turned in my work to a teacher who returned it with a grade, occasionally a comment. The importance of the work seemed to be singular: pleasing, or at least satisfying, the teacher. The larger world had no interest in or knowledge of my work. My friends didn't care about the quality of my work or even whether it was done. My family cared simply that the grades on my report card be good. The work I did was really a private affair.

There were rare occasions when my work was public and these moments carried an entirely different sense of pressure and impor-tance. Many decades later I still remember the times I worried about doing a good job: the time in second grade when I was cho-sen to paint a fish on the class ocean mural; the time in fourth grade when my friend and I sang a short solo in a Christmas concert; the times I was at bat in Little League baseball games; the times in high school I wrote articles for the school newspaper, played in soccer games, or acted in school plays. There was a reason to worry about quality in these settings: The world, or at least my world, was watching me. People cared about how well I did. I didn't want to let them down.

Every final draft my students complete is done for an outside audience. It may be for a small audience of Kindergarten children or for a national audience on educational television. Either way, my role as teacher is not as the sole judge of their work but rather similar to that of a sports coach or a play director: I am helping them to get their work ready for the public eye. *There is a reason to do the work well*, and it's not just because the teacher wants it that way.

When my students wrote biographies of senior citizens in town, no one needed to tell them the reason for doing a quality job. These books were to be gifts to the seniors, gifts that might become precious heirlooms for the seniors and their families. Each student held the life story of a senior in his or her hands. They were terribly nervous. Through weeks of interviews, with laughter, confusion, crankiness, and tears, student and seniors grew to trust each other. They shared cookies, stories, photographs, and sometimes hugs. When the time came to transform the interviews into books, I didn't need to remind students that spelling and neatness mattered: They wanted their books to be perfect. They agonized over the details and wanted critique and help from everyone. They read the first drafts of their opening paragraphs aloud to the whole class for suggestions. They labored, draft after draft, over the cover designs. After we photocopied the books, we presented the originals to our senior companions in an emotional ceremony.

When third and fourth graders in my school map amphibian habitats, tag monarch butterflies for state or national research efforts, or photograph historical sites in town for a book, when fifth and sixth graders monitor radon levels or water quality levels for the town, when Kindergartners make books and cards for senior citizens, all of them know their work makes a difference in the world.

Not every project or assignment can have life importance, but when students know that their finished work will be displayed, presented, appreciated, and judged—whether by the whole class, other classes, families, or the community—work takes on a different meaning. Many schools, my own included, have begun school traditions founded on sharing work. The Coalition of Essential Schools network has formalized such structures in schools across the country, based on the ideas of Ted Sizer and Deborah Meier. And, using inspiration from the Reggio Emilia pre-school work in Italy, my school makes an effort not just to document final products but also to document the learning process. In addition to final products, displays of work may include drafts of earlier work, evidence of discussion, and the ideas and strategies involved in the work's creation.

A few years ago I drove to Boston on a December evening to visit the Harbor School, an Expeditionary Learning Outward Bound middle school in Dorchester. It was their mid-year Exhibition Night. I had worked with the principal and teachers in the early days of this new public pilot school, and I was excited to see the student's work on display. I was greeted at the door by polite, well-dressed African American seventh graders who guided me upstairs with small smiles. Along with parents, siblings, relatives, ministers, city officials, administrators, teachers, and various members of the neighborhood, I toured the exhibition for an hour and a half. The community was dressed in their Sunday best and beaming with pride. They carried plates of fried chicken and potato salad, pie and cake. The school principal, my friend Scott Hartl, had spent the night before frantically installing and painting a gallery of black presentation boards that filled the auditorium and those boards were full of work. Every single child had work on display and each spoke articulately of the challenges and victories the work represented. This was hard, I heard over and over, this project was hard for me. I can't believe I got this done.

How do you start a new school and tell students who never before cared about the quality of their work that it's now time to care? Threaten them with poor grades? They've seen plenty of poor grades before. You give them a *reason* to care. The pressure of preparing for this *community* display, the daily focus on polishing work until it was worthy of presentation to the community—that was the reason this night.

I had some guests from Harvard in my classroom last year who wanted to talk with students. They had a particular request: They wanted to interview a student who hadn't been in the school the previous year. Cassie volunteered, and she spent quite a while with the group of educators in a corner of the room.

Over lunch I asked the guests what stood out about the interview. They said they had been curious as to how the culture of the school, different in so many ways from typical schools, would strike a student who was new to it. They had asked Cassie what the biggest difference was in this school, compared to her last. She told them that in this school her work was public. Everyone looked at her work; everyone cared about her work. In her old school only her teacher knew anything about her work. I have to try much harder in this school, she said, because the work is more important.

Using Assessment to Build Stronger Students

When the word *assessment* comes up, most people think of testing. Billions of dollars are spent annually in this country on testing—U.S. students are the most tested in the world—and the success or failure of schools and students is increasingly tied to the single skill of test taking. Oddly, test-taking skills have little connection to real life. When a student finishes schooling, she is judged for the rest of her life on the kind of person she is and the kind of work that she does. Rarely does this include how she performs on a test. When we assess the growth and progress of our own children, when we assess the value of our co-workers, it's not test scores but rather character and accomplishments that are the basis of our measure.

If tests are the primary measure of quality, the majority of schools feel compelled to have students spend much of their time memorizing facts and preparing for tests. These days a lot of politicians and newspaper editorials are asking the question: What's wrong with that? To many people, all this testing seems like a good idea. Well, it may make sense—until you consider the alternative: consider what we could have instead.

Imagine if students and schools were judged instead on the quality of student work, thinking, and character. Imagine an expectation that an adult should be able to enter a school and expect that any child in that school older than seven or eight would be ready to greet him politely, give an articulate tour of a well-maintained, courteous school environment, and present his portfolio of academic accomplishments clearly and insightfully, and that the student's portfolio would contain original, high-quality work and document appropriate skill levels. If schools assumed they were to going to be assessed by the quality of student behavior and work evident in the hallways and classrooms—rather than on test scores—the enormous energy poured into test preparation would be directed instead toward improving student work, understanding, and behavior. Instead of working to build clever test-takers, schools would feel compelled to spend time building thoughtful students and good citizens.

When I share these thoughts in public people always dismiss them as impractical. Sure it would be wonderful to actually look closely at schools and at student work, they say, but it's just not feasible. There's no time. Tests are the only feasible assessment system.

Here's something to consider: Many students at my school spend up to *three weeks* doing mandated testing. Not *preparing* for tests. *Taking* tests. The state has spent hundreds of million of dollars in the past few years developing and grading these tests, and who knows how much time. You could look at an awful lot in a school and an awful lot of student work in a awful lot of schools with this amount of time and money.

If schools went through the *quality review* process used in other countries and used by a number of school networks in this country, communities would get much more than a test score number. They would get a comprehensive report card on their school's ability to address its physical facilities, its staffing, its curriculum, its climate, its level of physical and emotional safety, its level of skill work, its quality of student achievement, and its assessment of the different school constituencies. If students developed and presented portfolios of their work, parents would get a clear picture of their child's skill levels, achievements, and learning style.

Most discussions of assessment start in the wrong place. The most important assessment that goes on in a school isn't done *to* students but goes on *inside* students. Every student walks around the school with a picture of what is acceptable, what is good enough. Each time he works on something he looks at it and assesses it. Is this good enough? Do I feel comfortable handing this in? Does it meet my standards? Changing assessment *at this level* should be the most important assessment goal of every school. How do we get inside students' heads and turn up the knob that regulates quality and effort? How do we affect self-assessment so that students have higher standards for their behavior and their work?

It's important to look at how assessment tools currently used in schools affect internalized standards. The strategy most often employed to create pressure for high standards is assigning grades to work. Ideally the promise of good grades and the threat of bad ones will keep everyone working hard. In reality, it doesn't always work this way. Almost every school gives grades and yet has no shortage of poor-quality work. Not only do grades not insure quality work or effort, but in many cases grades work against student motivation.

I'm not advocating abolishing grades, though my own school hasn't used them in twenty-five years and I believe it has contributed greatly to our effectiveness. I'm aware of the traditions and pressures for assigning grades. I'm suggesting that it's worth assessing the extent to which grades are used in a school, the extent to which children are ranked, the ways in which grades are derived in classrooms, and the extent to which reliance on grades have all created an *illusion* that genuine and effective assessment, particularly assessment which leads to improvement, is being done.

By the time I reached third grade as a public school student it was clear to me which students were the *good* students and got *good* grades and which students were the *bad* students who got *bad* grades. This hierarchy by grades earned indicated which students put effort into their work and which students had stopped trying and tended to horse around or sit silently. Other kids considered the low-grades group stupid; the low-grade earners spoke of themselves as stupid, and they let everyone know that they hated school. The kids who routinely got Cs and Ds all the time thought of themselves as C or D students. Why try? If these kids had already given up their effort in third grade, where would they be by the time they entered high school?

The school in which I teach has no C or D students. Some of the most talented and inspired scientific work performed as part of the water study project done two years ago in my classroom came from students who, due to learning disabilities, would have been D students in the schools of my youth. These students held no illusions concerning the degree of their learning challenges: They were painfully aware of their weaknesses, as almost all challenged children are. They were able, however, to work around their disabilities and, with learned strategies and support, produce quality work. They had strengths as thinkers and workers that were valuable, despite their academic challenges. When we hosted class guests, these students were as eager to present their portfolios as any child. They may have been struggling students but they were students with motivation and a strong work ethic.

If we have a grading system at my school it would have to be described as this: A piece of work deserves either an A or a Not Done. Work goes through many drafts and isn't considered complete until it represents high-quality work for that child. Any piece of work that would receive a C or D in a graded system is work not worthy of being accepted. Tests are the same way: If you do poorly on a test, you need to study and retake it until you do well.

I'm aware that it's difficult to rank students without quantifiable assessments, and I'm aware that there are times in the educational journey when it may be necessary to rank students. I'm not sure why we came to believe that we need to rank students every year, every week, almost every day. When we rank students on nationally normed tests it is unavoidable that 50 percent of them will fall into the *bottom-half* category. No parents want their kids to be in the bottom half, no teachers or administrators want their kids to be in the bottom half, but no matter what we do to improve education, half of America will always carry this discouraging identity. How many months or years of being a bottom-half student does it take to douse a child's spirit? Most educators and policy makers don't really understand the self-image and motivation problems that being a bottom-half student can bring, because almost every single one of them was in the top half—this may be why they chose education or government as a career.

Almost every school I consult with is required to give grades and my advice to them is this: Make sure the grades are seen by students as something they earn, rather than as the arbitrary decision of a teacher. Teachers who have rubrics of what constitutes an A or B on a specific assignment or for a quarter or semester: Allow students to decide to put in the work to earn an A instead of hoping for a good grade and complaining about a bad one. Ideally, students help to create those rubrics themselves. Allow students to redo work and retake tests until they earn a good grade rather than be branded by a poor one.

We have no easy replacement for grades at my school. We use a host of assessment strategies borrowed from all over. They're time consuming and complex and teachers always complain about the effort they take. We're committed to them anyway. Teachers conference with students continually and take notes on levels and qualities of reading, writing, and understanding. We use performance assessments—writing or solving problems on demand. We give tests that are numerically graded, but we require students to retake them until they score near the top. We have rubrics and checklists that students must fill out as they complete work, and we keep records of these. We have formal and informal presentations of particular projects and of general work portfolios, formal and informal critique sessions, and parent-student-teacher conferences during the year. Students regularly write self-assessments on particular projects or on general skill levels. We send home progress reports consisting of long narrative descriptions of student's strengths, weaknesses, learning styles, accomplishments, and goals. And we require students to take ownership of their own learning through keeping portfolios of work.

I have become a big fan of student portfolios. I have always saved samples of student work to share with parents, but fifteen years ago I learned from colleagues how to make portfolios alive and central in student learning, through consistent student sampling, analysis, and reflection.

I don't believe there is a single model for portfolios that suits everyone; I've encountered a variety of great models in my travels. I visited a Kindergarten in Tennessee where kids put all of their work in painted pizza boxes. All week long they stuffed their boxes with their paintings, drawings, writing, photographs of building block structures: all sorts of projects. On Friday morning in a sea of chaos they emptied out their boxes and sorted the work to take home. They chose one piece of work to share at portfolio meeting; the piece that they felt was their most important accomplishment of the week. I wandered through the room one Friday morning during the mass confusion and listened to fascinating discussions about which piece to choose, with students pouring over each other's work and giving advice. The sharing meeting was remarkable: Students this young were able to recognize and articulate important growth. A boy chose a drawing on which, for the first time, he had written his name correctly, and got cheers from the group. A girl showed a drawing of her sneakers and explained that the picture wasn't the accomplishment but the fact that she had learned to tie her shoes, finally, that week was. Another girl showed a photo of herself with another girl in the dress-up corner and mentioned that her best accomplishment that week had been making a new friend, as making new friends was hard for her.

I visited a high school in Montana where every student kept a portfolio of his or her accomplishments in all realms. The portfolios included an autobiography, a resume, records of all classes taken and grades earned, work samples from every discipline, important projects and research papers, and evidence of achievements in arts, sports, and service. Every student presented his or her portfolio formally to a panel each year with pride.

I met the director of instrumental music for a district in Massachusetts who had instituted a simple and wonderful portfolio assignment for each student taking music lessons. Every few months the student would sit in front of a tape recorder and play a short, *original* composition. The student would then describe why he wrote it and played it that way. The system took almost no work on the part of the music instructors except turning on the tape player and storing the tapes.

He played a sample portfolio. It began with the voice of a little child introducing a squeaky saxophone piece consisting of only a few notes. The child explained that he wrote the piece this way because he only knew a few notes; I think it was a variation of "Three Blind Mice." Subsequent entries showed his increasing sophistication. He played original compositions that became more and more complex, and spoke articulately about his growth and the composition process—how he chose themes and titles for his pieces, how he set moods, and how he chose to open and close his pieces. Finally his much matured student voice introduced a challenging jazz composition that he explained was influenced by John Coltrane. I was stunned.

I look forward to a time when students wouldn't think of going to a college interview or job interview without a portfolio of their work and accomplishments in hand. And to a time when rather than spending their years in school accruing hours and seat-time so they can pass to the next year and graduate, students will think always of what they've accomplished so far and of what comes next. Some of the small high schools that have embraced Central Park East's model have a culture like this already. The students feel the work is important, they know their work will be made public, and they feel responsible for documenting their own learning. These schools' records of sending kids on to college—kids from neighborhoods where to be acceptable to a college is an uncommon event—are remarkable.

A Classroom Story: The Water Study

I'm standing in a shaded woodland stream, the current reaching almost to my knees, and the September morning sun filters through the trees in small patches on the water. It doesn't seem possible the water is as cold as it is; autumn has just begun and already the weeds are laced with morning frost, melting where the sun touches. In front of me a fifth-grade girl, Rachel, and a sixth-grade boy, Conan, are crouched on the bank oblivious to the cold, consumed in scientific concentration. They are clad in sweatshirts, laboratory goggles, and rubber gloves, titrating drops of acid into a small vial to test the dissolved oxygen content of the stream water. They count their drops carefully, watching the solution, nervous. A bad reading will mean that the stream does not contain enough oxygen to support the fish and crayfish that should be living here. No one has tested this stream before; we have no idea what we'll find. Rachel keeps reassuring us—I'm sure the water is fine; all these streams have fish—as she tries to reassure herself. They pour the solution into a holding container and get out their notebooks quickly to calculate the reading. They look up from their notebooks with broad smiles of relief. It's fine, they say. It's really good.

Three years ago I had as high a percentage of special education students in my classroom as I've had in twenty-five years. Many of these students had never scored high on a standardized test and probably never will. Yet they accomplished a scientific work profound by anyone's standards, that I would be pleased to see students in any school in America do—elementary, middle, or high school. When their research was published and shared both locally and nationally, they graduated sixth grade with something special: copies of their scientific reports which were now a part of the town archives, copies of newspaper and magazine articles on their work, individual copies of a video documentary done on their work for television, and the memory of having done something important to help their community.

The project began one spring evening with a phone call from my old friend John Reid, geology professor at Hampshire College. As usual, I got roped into an investigation far beyond my expertise and understanding. His enthusiasm was once again irresistible.

Ronnie, he boomed, I've got a new machine! This was trouble, I knew. Last time John got a new machine I was dragged into a project that took months of intensive work—The Radon Study. I knew the radon research was one of the most exciting and valuable things I'd done with students, but still, I didn't forget for a moment how worried and overwhelmed I was for months, or all the panic and confusion caused. I was clear with him this time. John, I just can't take on a project like last time.

He didn't seem to hear me. He just kept going. What a machine! It's an Inductively Coupled Plasma Mass Spectrometer. We can test the water in your town and do a spectral analysis of what's in it. With your students gathering well samples from all over, think of what we can discover! Nobody tests their water for all these elements, nobody. Think of the patterns we might find! Think of what a service this would be to the community: We can test for metals in their drinking water.

I was still digesting the name *Inductively Coupled Plasma Mass Spectrometer.* Though my students could later easily pronounce the name of this machine (which costs three times as much as my house) and could even draw diagrams of its interior and describe its function in elegant, simple language, at that time I was a bit overwhelmed. Of course, John said, it's a very delicate machine and goes down all the time, so keeping to a schedule can be difficult, and it will cost a few thousand dollars to run your town's water samples on it. Of course, I thought. No problem. I'll ask the students to bring in a couple thousand dollars to get us started and tell them to touch the machine very gently.

In the end there was no resisting John. The technology teacher at my school and I wrote a grant proposal to the state and the thousands of dollars needed to run the machine became real. Now all I had to do before the fall was to learn what the heck this machine was and take a crash course in hydrology and water chemistry so that I had some idea what we would be doing. It was a busy summer. When I wasn't building or working with teachers, I was visiting water experts and asking for their guidance. That summer and throughout the fall semester I leaned on the expertise of others to make this project possible. Even with research I felt continually over my head, so to speak, with this water study, and succeeded through the kindness of scientists and educators from all over.

A scientist named Clif Read, the parent of a former student, worked for a state water commission. He not only patiently taught me the basics but also loaned me piles of books, surface water test kits, demonstration models, and volunteered to teach students in the classroom and to accompany us in some of our outdoor research. He had a cartographer in his office prepare for us, free of charge, wall-sized GIS topographic maps of our town. In the fall, these maps were covered with colored pins and looked like the giant crime maps of Hollywood movie police stations.

Before we could take on the spectral analysis of well water in town homes, I learned that I had better start the kids off with a less complex scientific task. We planned the first stage of the water project. We would test the town's surface water—streams and lakes—for pollution. We would do this with inexpensive test kits designed for high school chemistry classes, and the amount of data generated would not be overwhelming.

We spent many crisp days in the streams underneath autumn trees, testing for pH, turbidity, nitrates, dissolved oxygen, and other indicators of stream health. A few people questioned whether kids this young, particularly some of my behaviorally challenged fifth grade boys, were mature enough to handle delicate scientific equipment and dangerous acids. It never surfaced as a concern. All the students, boys and girls alike, were meticulous in their care and respect for the testing equipment. In small, mixed-gender, mixed-age teams, outfitted in goggles and gloves, they worked with serious precision.

John Reid loaned us two talented college students to help with experimental procedures and data analysis. One of these students, Jessica Harris, visited off and on for months, helping students troubleshoot their Microsoft Excel spreadsheet problems, import digital photographs into their text, and helping them build a project website. Students worked in small teams analyzing results and each team was responsible for writing a section of the report. Although these sections were brief they took many days, even weeks, to complete. Some of them went through ten or twelve drafts. Students learned that good data analysis and scientific writing take time.

When the report was completed and presented to town boards and the local media, there was a celebration of pride in the classroom. Every student had shared an important role in the project. A student with profound reading and writing learning disabilities was one of the strongest in the class in computer-based data analysis. A student with a serious medical syndrome that made much schoolwork impossible had been very competent in the field, completing water tests with real understanding. The class knew it was ready to take on the more complex analysis of drinking water—the testing of private wells in town using the mass spectrometer.

Once the well project began, the classroom was transformed. The days were filled with preparing maps, surveys, data forms, instruction sheets; labeling and packing sterile bottles and test kits; planning meetings, developing distribution protocols and testing schedules. There were lessons in science, math, writing, technology, and politics—all needed for the project—and there were many formal critique sessions. Much of the time, however, students came in to school, checked in like workers in a business, and got down to work writing, editing, organizing, packing, and preparing endless graphs and tables. Many days I had to force them to leave the computers and get to lunch. Students worked both at school and at the college laboratory. Students who had never been in a college, whose families had never considered college, worked in a college lab with undergraduates and professors.

Did they take this work seriously? You bet they did. People's health depended on their accuracy. The whole town, and lots of nervous families, were anxiously awaiting their findings. When we got our first data sheets with test results, each child in class analyzed the results of a particular family well in order to prepare a report for the family. We were about fifteen minutes into the study analyses when one boy noticed a level of a metallic element that was above federal standards. He began to cry. Other students gathered around him. Though we had discussed this for weeks and had memorized federal standards exactly for this purpose, it took on a new meaning when it was real data. This was a family's drinking water; this affected the life of a Kindergartner in our school, a boy we knew and loved.

The students wrote individual letters to every family. The letters contained personal well results and explanations of what the results meant. The letters contained background information on any elements of concern in the water and explanations of how particular problems could be addressed. As I live in town, I was on the list like everyone else. I received a letter congratulating me on having no elemental levels in my water that represented health concerns but informing me that there were levels of iron and manganese in my water that exceeded federal guidelines; the letter explained the possible problems that this could cause.

The class then chose research questions based on the results. Again we split into teams to look for patterns and relationships in the data. This would be the basis of our town report and website.

During the course of this study we were visited by a film crew that was preparing a documentary on exemplary science projects across the country. They spent a day interviewing students and filming classroom work sessions. Two weeks later we received by mail five hours of raw footage showing a day in the life of our project.

(Here's some advice. Don't ever watch yourself or your classroom on videotape for five hours. Have you ever looked at a photograph of yourself and thought: I can't possibly look that bad . . . that's not what I look like, is it? Well, I had five hours of that feeling.)

There were some great moments. These are true: Two boys creating a scatter plot on the computer and cheering and dancing when the pattern they predicted appeared on the screen. We're good. We're good, they chanted. Class presentations of data by research teams with great critique by students and heated discussions of the results. Much of what the student research teams were finding went against all of our predictions; what the heck was going on? We were finding high levels of lead in the water of new homes, homes built after the elimination of lead solder for pipes. We knew it wasn't coming from the ground. Where in the world was this lead coming from? The confusion and excitement of real research was very plain. There was a sweet scene of a little boy and girl sitting together underneath a table, patiently, carefully labeling envelopes as the class bustled above and around them. All of the students who were individually interviewed on film were, thankfully, knowledgeable, articulate, and poised.

But, honestly, five hours of intense student work—sometimes tedious, often noisy—didn't exactly make exciting viewing. I couldn't imagine how this tape could be useful to someone.

I took the tapes to school and played them in the corner of the room one day while we were working on our research. For ten minutes the students were enthralled to see themselves on television. But soon they drifted away and the tapes droned on in the background. At the end of five hours the class agreed that it was the most boring videotape ever recorded in human history.

A month later we received in the mail an edited version of the videotape. It was no longer five hours. Eight minutes and fifty-one seconds—our portion of an hour documentary. We watched the tape. Except for Maria, who was appalled at what she was wearing in her interview, the class thought that our project and our classroom looked fantastic. The students wrote to the documentary crew and requested individual copies of the tape so that each student could own a copy to use for portfolio presentations and to show their families. One boy said he was saving it to use in his college interview. And I was heartened to think there were at least nine minutes, or almost nine minutes, of a typical day in my classroom that were well done.

The maturity the students exhibited during this study floored me. The data we handled were ethically and emotionally charged—this was confidential health information about homes in town. Never once in the course of the research was there a suggestion of a student compromising this confidence. When results from certain houses raised student concerns, the class got involved in deep and sensitive discussions of how to best inform and support the families receiving troubling news. The results of one home well of one Kindergarten student were so puzzling and concerning that students requested more information from the family. (It turned out that the alarming copper sample was taken from a laundry faucet that had not been used for a long time; the high copper level was caused by leaching during that period.) Students handled high school, college, and professional scientific equipment for months without a problem. They worked collaboratively with college students and professors politely and appropriately in the field and in the lab.

I was continually impressed with the students' self-sufficiency. I will never forget a morning when Julia and Maria told me their research section was complete and they were ready for a new task. I was too distracted to give a good reply. I held up a booklet of members of town boards and officials, and mentioned that we needed to begin composing individual letters to them summarizing our findings and including an explanation of the general report. They left for the computer lab with the booklet and I resumed my critique with another team. About two and a half hours later I noticed that Julia and Maria were not in the room; in fact, they had missed a group critique session and were about to miss a math lesson on data analysis. Where were they? Carl knew: They're in the computer lab, he said, I'll get them. They returned with piles of envelopes hand-lettered in beautiful calligraphy addressed to members of the town boards. In each envelope was an individual word-processed business letter tailored to that board. I read through the letters: They were appropriate in form, layout, and mechanics; they were polite, clear, and scientifically accurate. I would have assumed that an adult would have taken a day or two to accomplish this. I felt a little guilty that they weren't on salary.

The project took months. Shouldn't we instead have been covering fifty or sixty of the hundreds of new state requirements (*standards*) and memorizing facts for tests? When the state department of education came to see how their grant money was being spent, they may have brought checklists to insure we were covering the state standards, but I didn't see any. As soon as the state officials spoke with students and looked at the research they had one question: May we return with a film crew? We became one of a handful of programs featured on a promotional state video about use of technology in the classroom. Do I regret sacrificing the shallow coverage of countless facts in order to have students craft something of excellence and importance? Not for a moment. Many of these students hope to become scientists. In fact, as Maria said to her fellow students, We already are!

Last year I was at the check out counter of a grocery store and the cashier, the mother of one of the students who worked on the project, looked at me and said: My son will never be the same. No matter how many tests tell him he's stupid, he knows he's not. He did that work. He knows he's capable of excellence.

CHAPTER FOUR

The Third Toolbox
Teaching of Excellence

Supporting Teachers

It's a brighter Saturday morning for our teacher group, no rain or snow today. No one seems worried today about the angry principal. One positive thing about old school buildings is the tall windows and today some sunshine is tentatively reaching down into the staff room. The table is filled with the modest breakfast of public school teachers—no corporate brunch here—cartons of orange juice, plastic cups, styrofoam coffee cups with lids, boxes of minidonuts, paper napkins.

Today teachers have brought early efforts at projects by their students. Since we began meeting there's been progress. The work is modest but the teachers are proud. It's a beginning. The students are excited, they say. We look at the work together and give comments.

At first the comments are compliments, which is fine. This is a good place to begin—everyone needs affirmation here. Then I try to gently lead the group into constructive criticism: How do we make this work stronger? What strategies can we use to do so? Teachers have begun using critique sessions in their classrooms but this is the first time they've made their own work as teachers public, open to critique from their peers.

We go around the group one-by-one, focusing on each teacher. The presenting teacher shares and explains work from her class-room. The suggestions from colleagues are quite good; I'm impressed. There are lots of useful comments and strategies offered. I add my own for each teacher. Remarkably, none of the presenters gets defensive. They listen carefully and most of them take notes about the comments they get.

We spend time brainstorming plans for a spring exhibition of work: regular education students, special education students, and bilingual students all working together preparing work for the public. We need a structure that will fit easily into the cur-ricular demands of each classroom because the pressure to *cover* topics is so great. We decide on an Author's Night. The commu-nity and the press will be invited to the school to see books and meet the authors, the authors being all of the students. Each student will complete a polished, final-draft book to be on dis-play that evening and will be rehearsed and prepared to speak about it.

The group decides not to standardize the subject of the books. Some books will be fiction, some non-fiction; each teacher wants the freedom to focus the book topics to fit in with what she is study-ing with her class. What will be common to all of these projects are the standards for the finished artifacts, the format of the evening, and the rehearsals for presentations. The group is excited at the prospect.

I look at this group of teachers and I'm filled with admiration. The building is a wreck, the administration is awful, the students are transient and struggling, the newspapers attack the school and the teachers with criticism over test scores. But these people aren't giving up!

Architects of school reform need to have a builder's breakfast like the ones we have sometime. If schools are to improve it must begin here with the teachers. We can pass laws and mandate tests and new standards and anything we want, but it's not going to do much if we can't support teachers.

Teaching as a Calling

In twenty-five years of teaching I've taken off two years. After eight years in the classroom I took a leave of absence to work full-time as a carpenter. It was a valuable year for me in a number of ways. I was able to put aside some savings for my family that I hadn't been able to do on a teacher's salary. I had the chance to put my full heart into improving my building skills and knowledge of my craft. And I had an extended opportunity to reflect on the teaching world.

My days were long and often hard, and not all the work was pleasant. I was on my back in August heat insulating a crawl space beneath a house addition, fiberglass particles raining down on my sweaty face; I was up on a snowy slate roof in the January wind, holding on to the ridge cap as I worked. Nevertheless my primary feeling that year was one of profound relief and rest. The responsibility of all those kids and families depending on me; the relentless neccessity to be *on* every morning, smiling and organized, ready for all those young faces; the harried schedule allowing almost no time to think or eat lunch; the pressure of worrying whether I was clear enough, firm enough, sensitive enough, whether I was inspiring and helping each student as I should. All of these were gone.

As a builder, I could go into work quiet and unshaven, spend a morning by myself carefully building a stair balustrade in a peaceful, sun-lit corner of a beautiful old house. I could go in late, if needed, or not at all. I had no sense of terror at the thought of a struggling substitute teacher possibly undermining some of my hard work spent building a polite, safe classroom community. I could build things of wood and trust with confidence that they would last; the gains I made with students often seemed ephemeral and fragile. I could go home in the evenings and have a calm dinner with my family, and relax with them afterwards instead of going upstairs to my desk to do schoolwork. Perhaps best of all: I could sleep deeply and soundly, a delicious sleep untroubled by lessons and children's needs and worried faces.

Something struck me that year: Teaching is hard. Harder than I can ever explain to anyone. Doing it well, consistently, takes a unique stamina. I didn't really see that until I took a breather and realized how fast I'd been running. For anyone with talent and options, choosing to enter teaching and giving up the money, flexibility, and respect that so many other careers offer in order to take on the stress of the classroom is just crazy. Unless you see teaching as a calling. Unless you feel that teaching is what you are intended for; that it is your way to share the best of what you have to give to the world.

I knew I had to return. I loved working with kids. I was blessed with an ideal setting in which to pursue my teaching practice: I had found a school that brought out the best in me. My colleagues were inspirational. My administration supported the teachers to handcraft a curriculum and culture that worked. We shared a common vision that centered on children. The community trusted us. The days might be exhausting but we didn't need to compromise our vision: We could be passionate, creative, and obsessive about quality. Even with all the stress I felt fortunate to have that opportunity.

What can schools do to recruit and keep teachers who are passionate and talented? Here's my opinion: Forget the gimmicks, the signing bonuses, the merit pay, the special titles. All the financial bonuses added together generally won't come close to the salary increase a talented teacher will realize in the very first year of a career change into the corporate world. Instead, assume that strong teachers do view their profession as a calling and that what they want most is an environment that respects and supports the growth of their teaching practice. To attract talented young people into teaching, the first step must be offering a salary structure that acknowledges the importance of the profession. Currently, teaching salaries are so meager compared to the corporate world that very few top students even consider teaching as a career. The average education major in America is a below-average college student. But improved salaries alone won't solve the problem. A strong teacher won't stay in the profession very long unless she is given the time, respect, resources, and support necessary to be proud of her work.

Almost half of America's new teachers leave the profession within five years. That the pay is often terrible is not even the worst part. These teachers struggle in isolated settings, often without support, trust, or respect. They are quickly overwhelmed and soon disheartened. That is the worst part.

Sometimes I visit a public school where the climate is more positive. It may be a pilot school or a charter school or simply a school with a strong community or visionary administrator. There is a profound difference there: The teachers feel respected. They are trusted to plan curriculum, to plan their day, to try out new ideas; they are supported to work together. They don't spend their days in the teacher's room discussing retirement or searching for other jobs.

Teachers want a work schedule that honors their need for time for planning, preparation, reflection, research, and collaboration. They want to trust that their professional expertise in decisions of curriculum, instruction, and school culture will be sought out and taken seriously. They want support with the needy children and families that worry them at night. They want professional respect and growth to be integral to their work. And they want some breathing room: The endless layers of state, district, school, and department requirements can leave little time or opportunity for them to make professional decisions about what works best with students.

During the past five years, a large portion of the gifted teachers I know, many of them recipients of prestigious teaching awards, have left the profession prior to retirement, in favor of more rewarding pursuits. Almost all have left in sadness and frustration. As "solutions" to the education "crisis" are dreamed up by the political and educational bureaucracy, mandates have taken away from teachers more and more of the opportunities for creativity and inspiration in the classroom. These teachers, their days eaten up by new, conflicting requirements, their work now judged almost entirely on test scores, could compromise their standards no more. The idea that new merit bonuses of a few thousand dollars could lure back such teachers—professionals who have given up perhaps half a million dollars in career income dedicating their lives to working with children—is a tragic example of how little those in power understand the source of teacher dedication.

The second year I took off from teaching was after I spent fifteen years in the classroom. I entered a master's degree program in which I had the unique opportunity to study under noted educator and writer Howard Gardner. I was able to arrange my spring semester schedule so that I could work with the research group he supervised: Harvard Project Zero. That spring, with the guidance of Project Zero researchers Steve Seidel and Dennie Wolf, I designed an independent study project.

The structure of the study was simple: I wanted to visit good schools and good classrooms. I agreed to discuss and record my findings. I asked almost everyone—my colleagues and connections in education, my friends and family, and even people I met at parties—a simple question. Did they know of any outstanding schools, programs, or individual teachers that I should visit. It didn't matter what age level or context; I would follow any lead.

I got on the phone with a speech prepared for each school. I said I was at Harvard researching outstanding schools and teachers and I was given their name. I was hoping to arrange a visit. Now all of this was true and it sounded better than saying I was a teacher who had been hiding in the woods for fifteen years and was excited to borrow ideas and inspiration from great classrooms. I was soon in my truck driving all over the state and the region. It was remarkable. One day I was at an inner-city pre-school classroom in the basement of a church annex, sounds of traffic and construction blaring through the milky Plexiglas windows; the next day I was at an elite preparatory school, walking across vast, quiet lawns with an admissions tour guide dressed in a blue blazer with gold buttons. Wherever I was I eventually ended up in a classroom in which I would marvel at the artistry of a great teacher connecting with students. I walked down hallways and opened doors into secret kingdoms, worlds suffused by the particular genius and magic of that teacher.

I saw strange things that year. I saw a high school classroom in a large, all-black city school that was decorated like a soda fountain from the 1950s. Or perhaps it was decorated like a Valentine's Party, except that the party never ended. In a school that was dark and run-down, gang graffiti on its outside walls, metal detectors at its front door, this room was bright and sunny with red and white checkered tablecloths on little round work tables, real flowers on the counter, red paper and doilies on the walls, student work displayed everywhere in festive, artistic arrangements. I would have imagined high school kids would have laughed at these cute decorations but I couldn't have been more wrong. Even the gang members, I was told by a girl in class, took off their hats respectfully when they entered this sanctuary. The English classes I observed were interrupted frequently by students poking their heads in the door to admire the classroom; often they called out before disappearing: I love this classroom! or Why can't I be in this class?

I saw a second-grade classroom in which students were reading on the beach. A truckload of sand had been dumped in a corner of the room that had been framed with wood. Behind it was a mural of the ocean and sky painted by students, and the sand was sprinkled with shells, rocks, and driftwood collected by the students on their trips to the seashore. Basking under the warm glow of clamp lights, a group of students did their silent reading on beach chairs or blankets, undisturbed by my visit to the their seaside world.

I observed the classroom of a gifted fifth-grade teacher who told me that down the hallway was another teacher I just had to meet. If you like my classroom, she said, you'll love hers: We're just the same. I went down the hallway and found myself in a room that couldn't have been more different from the room I had just left. The first teacher had been a young white woman, easy and loose with the children, her classroom a mess of projects and artwork. The second teacher was an older African American woman, stern and tough, whose room was spotless with desks in straight rows. I was impressed with both, but totally confused. I had lunch with both of them, and found that they were friends and viewed each other as having identical visions of teaching. I asked them what they possibly viewed as their common vision.

They talked all through lunch. This is what I heard them say: Teaching isn't about papers and pencils; teaching is about relationships. We try to visit our students at their homes before the year begins. Both of us keep in close touch with parents. Both of us get to know every child really well, because all the power we have to get that child to be more confident and successful comes from knowing him or her well. How can you push a child to do better work unless you know exactly what her best work looks like and where it can be improved? Lots of teachers here just teach by the book but we teach from the heart. We love our students and they love us back. Not all of our colleagues like us because they think we work too hard and parents always request our classrooms, but this is the only way we can teach.

When I observed the artistry of teachers using their relationships with individual students and groups to inspire, to challenge, to push, to cultivate growth and confidence, I saw clearly how much of my own power as a teacher was predicated on my relationships with students and my ability to shape a culture in which peer relationships were a positive social and academic force.

The teachers who made a difference in my own life knew how to support me and how to push me: They used their personal relationship with me, whether warm and casual or formal and intimidating, in a masterful way. These relationships became a conduit through which their passion for learning and subject knowledge became mine. Most adults I've spoken with remember a teacher, or a few teachers, with whom they had a powerful relationship, a teacher who had a deep impact on their lives.

This may all seem like old news but I'm concerned that it's often forgotten these days. Ten years after those classroom visits, I was presenting at a conference in Washington, D.C. The conference was focused primarily on how to improve achievement levels in inner-city schools and on how to break the cycle of academic inequity for minority children. The solution in the air was not stronger teachers but rather to *teacher-proof* education.

My co-presenter was my friend and colleague Evelyn Jenkins Gunn, an award-winning teacher from New York. On the surface Evelyn and I could hardly be more different. She is an African American woman who grew up in the Deep South and now teaches high school English at a school outside of New York City. I am a white man who grew up in the North who teaches elementary school in the middle of the New England woods. As Carnegie Teaching Scholars we were able to spend parts of three summers together researching our practice with a small group of colleagues from around the country. We found that we were, underneath, very much alike. We shared a common vision of standards and expectations for students, and a love for students, which made us feel like old friends.

The conference participants were charged: they were impatient for change, and understandably so. Urban students had been neglected by society for too long; it was time for sweeping legislative change to end the injustice. I admired their passion but I was concerned about their vision. They wanted a short cut. They wanted to *legislate* that every child would achieve, be successful. We need tests, they felt, more tests and rigid cut-offs for promotion. We need laws and rules that no school can avoid. They wanted *teacher-proof* curriculum: systems not dependent on the variable quality of instructors and that could be *delivered* efficiently. They wanted to bypass teaching altogether and mandate that students would *receive* the proper amount of material. They wanted *systems* for *delivering material* that could be codified, measured, and scaled-up right away.

I admired their mission and their zeal; I empathized with their impatience. But their notion of education was to *put material into kid's heads.* There was no discussion of students constructing understanding, making discoveries, thinking critically. No one pointed out that in the top ranking schools much of the curriculum centers on developing the skills needed to obtain high-level jobs, skills beyond memorization, nor did anyone mention that the teaching in these prestigious schools is top-notch and the teachers are revered. Urban children of color deserve the same.

Evelyn and I looked around at lunch and realized that of all the people attending this conference on how to improve education, we were just about the only teachers. The keynote address that morning had taken over an hour and the word *teaching* was never mentioned nor was the word *teacher* used. When some participants learned that I was a teacher they were politely dismissive: No offense, but we don't need any more hero teachers, they said. We don't need more Jaime Escalantes and Teachers of the Year. There will always be a few great teachers around proving the point that the current system can work. But mostly it doesn't: It's broken; It's failed minority children. We can't a base a system for urban education on teachers; There are few good ones around. *We need a system that is teacher independent.*

When Evelyn began her part of our presentation she showed artifacts from her youth—a tattered book, a photograph of the tiny country shack in which she and her many siblings grew up. She said to the audience: I am here today because of a teacher. I defied the odds because there was a special, powerful woman who believed in me, who touched my heart, who taught us it didn't matter if we were poor or black or ugly or small: She taught us to be successful. I am a nationally recognized professional speaking at a conference because of this woman who changed my life.

Evelyn was a model of exactly what this conference was all about—how to transform those with little hope into those determined to find success, how to show a black child from a poor family a pathway to a distinguished life. I only prayed those in the audience would hear her message: It was a *teacher* who turned her life around.

Teaching as a Craft

Carpenters learn their craft in a sensible manner. They spend years on the job as apprentices and journeymen before they are considered masters. Independence and responsibility are granted slowly as young carpenters labor under the watchful eyes of experienced builders. They prove themselves not by taking tests but by demonstrating good work skills, high quality standards and a strong work ethic. They are taught by the entire crew.

Imagine that a carpenter fresh from school was sent to build your house. He had read carpentry books and had taken lots of tests but had spent only a few months on an actual building site and had been given real responsibility on that site for just a single week. Not only that, he was going to build your house entirely by himself, with no one collaborating with him, guiding his work, or watching over his decisions. You'd be out of your mind if you felt comfortable with this arrangement. How did it come to be that we send our children to first-year teachers with this type of preparation? Who dreamed up a system in which teachers fresh from college with no real experience whatsoever are immediately given a level of responsibility as great as they will ever have in their teaching career?

The system America has for introducing individuals to and then supporting them in the craft of teaching makes no sense to me. The years of apprenticeship that carpenters go through must be shortened to months or even weeks to be comparable with the system of teacher preparation. You'd think kids would be considered at least as important as houses.

Builders receive guidance for years from the master builders on the crew; sometimes the guidance lasts a lifetime. My building partner and I frequently consult with each other. Teachers are left alone in a classroom. *First year teachers* are left alone in a classroom. Even in schools with recently established mentor programs, the mentor is far away in another classroom—another world. Most first-year teachers struggle to develop management systems and instruction strategies; many fall back on systems and strategies from their own past even if those strategies didn't work particularly well. Teachers often hold onto these strategies insecurely for the next year, perhaps thirty more. The isolation of their classroom is often viewed sadly as a blessing: feeling that they're not doing well enough, they hope to be left alone and never observed. They take pride in the success of individual students but feel that the class as a whole should be doing better. They cling to what's familiar and are threatened by new ideas or strategies; when forced to attend staff development workshops they can only talk about why new ideas won't work.

I'm painting here a bleak portrait of teachers, and it certainly doesn't apply to all. But my work with staffs around the country has made it painfully clear to me how many teachers have become isolated, self-protective, and insecure.

When I worked evenings as an instructor at a local university's teacher education program, the limits of our preparation model were particularly clear to me. The faculty in the school of education was talented, and I for one certainly gave my full heart to my students, future teachers. But one can't learn to teach sitting in a classroom any more than one can learn to build houses sitting in a classroom. When I ran into one of my former university students years later—she was teaching at a school I visited—I asked her about the preparation she received at the university. The teachers were great there, she said, but when I got into the classroom I didn't really know how to teach. I had hardly practiced teaching at all . . . I didn't know what to do a lot of the time. And there was no one to ask . . .

It doesn't have to be this way. My Japanese friends in graduate school had an entirely different view of the profession. They were returning to Japan to jobs for which they were well paid, relative to other professions; jobs in which they were highly respected, even honored, by their communities. They spoke of the reverent way they were greeted in public. They received continual help from colleagues on the job. Compared to American teachers they had a great deal of planning time and opportunities to collaborate with other teachers during their teaching day. Frequently their lessons were observed by colleagues or they observed others teaching in order to share good instructional strategies. Master teachers were role models for younger ones.

There are glimmers of hope in this country. Some districts are beginning to offer teachers salaries that are more comparable to those offered in the business world. Many states are beginning to view mentor programs for first-year teachers as an important idea. But we have a long way to go. One year my daughter made as much waitressing in a nice restaurant as I did teaching full-time, and when she opened a catering business her income passed mine easily. Few experienced teachers I know have volunteered to be a mentor teacher because even though there is often a stipend attached, the operating structure is unworkable. Unlike in a carpentry apprenticeship, the "apprentice" teachers struggle alone; they're not assigned to team teach with a master teacher. Yet they still bear the same degree of responsibility as their mentor teacher. The mentor teachers are expected to carry a full teaching load and, in addition, find the time to observe, guide, support, and teach an apprentice teacher who is in a different classroom. Most teachers barely have time to run to the bathroom let alone run to another classroom to help another teacher.

We need a lot of teachers in this country and we need a constant supply of new ones. To keep this supply flowing, there are two paths we can take. The first is to make the job highly desirable: good salary, good working conditions, viewed with respect. Many strong college students would be drawn to it and hiring standards could be high. Teacher preparation would include a long, effective apprenticeship: years on the job with guidance from experienced professionals. By the time a beginning teacher was truly independent he or she would be solid, confident, and inclined to stay in the field.

The second path is much less expensive in the short run. Forget the good salary, the respect, the favorable working conditions; just make it easy to become a teacher. Have low hiring standards and a quick certification process with no expensive internship period. Lots of college students without clear direction or options would be drawn to teaching; they could be dumped into classrooms alone immediately after graduation. If half of them soon quit, we could always replace them with more cheap labor.

It's clear to me which of these paths we've opted for. It's worth considering the price we pay in the long run.

The Scholarship of Teaching

It's not such a crazy idea, thinking of teachers as scholars. In fact, in prestigious American schools and in those of other countries in which teachers actually view themselves as scholars, the quality of teaching is generally superb.

There is nothing new in the idea of teacher scholars: In America there is a heritage of teachers researching their own practice by documenting their work, writing about their work, observing the work of others, and comparing best practices. In some countries this view is the norm: Most articles published in education magazines in these countries are written not by researchers in universities but by classroom teachers investigating their own practices.

The problem is that not too many people in the United States are even aware of the notion of teacher scholarship. Few public school teachers are supported or encouraged to engage in scholarship centered around their practice, and few administrators or policy makers have any idea of the power of scholarship in improving instructional practice. While working with the Carnegie Foundation over the past few years, I have sat in on many discussions about how the scholarship of teaching should be defined. I'm not sure there will ever be consensus on an exact definition but I'm convinced that it's a powerful and important movement.

In the past ten years I've had the privilege of spending time with many teachers who are investigating their practice. The excitement and knowledge that they develop is universal. These teachers were researching or documenting their practice for presentations given at conferences or to professional work groups sponsored by Expeditionary Learning Outward Bound, The National Writer's Project, The National Council of Teachers of Mathematics, The Coalition of Essential Schools, and similar networks, or for national board certification. They are teachers who take their work seriously. Just like with students, the pressure that comes with making their work public compels them to put unusual effort and thoughtfulness into their practice.

The first Saturday of each month I get up early and drive across the state to attend a meeting of teachers who get together to look closely at student work and discuss what it means to teach. Run by Steve Seidel at Project Zero, the group uses Steve's Collaborative Assessment critique protocol to analyze a piece of schoolwork, and also listens to teachers share projects they feel to be particularly successful or provocative. Teachers and administrators attend these meetings for one purpose: to reflect together. There is no money, no credit, and no external reward given for showing up. Anyone can come and everyone has equal status in the group. People travel from all over. Most are from the Boston area but I've met educators there from Maine, New York City, Ohio, Italy, and South America. People come just for the opportunity to sit in a circle and discuss student work; they have been doing so for almost ten years.

In my work with Expeditionary Learning and The Coalition of Essential Schools, network conferences are built around a core of teacher presentations. Teachers from participating schools lead workshops in which they share the struggles and successes of particular projects or of their practice in general. Many school networks use this model, with good reason. I've spent a great deal of time helping teachers refine their instruction and curriculum strategies, and I can say there are few motivators as powerful to a teacher as knowing that he will be presenting his success—or lack of success—with students to a critical public.

One of the "wake-up calls" to U.S. education that I read about frequently is how American secondary students compare internationally, and in particular to Asian students in the areas of science and math. U.S. test scores have often been disappointing. The fix has been to cram more required topics into a curriculum that is too crowded already. However, it would be more useful to analyze what's going on in countries that score well. Catherine Lewis, an American researcher who is a specialist in Japanese education, gives a compelling description of how effective Japanese schools are quite different from how we may picture them.

The average eighth-grade Japanese science textbook has just eight topics, compared to the sixty-five found in the average U.S. textbook. By covering less and learning it more deeply, students have "plenty of time for hands on exploration." With less material to cover, teachers devote much of their time to researching their practice: studying the most effective ways to present the material and concepts. Collaboration between teachers is the norm, as is observing each other's lessons. Because the Japanese attribute success more to hard work than ability, for both students and teachers, teachers can continue to improve their practice by studying the lessons of others. Lewis quotes a Japanese teacher: "Our textbooks are very thin, with few explanations . . . Teachers have to fill in the blanks between the lines about lessons . . . Unless you improve your own skills, you can't teach a good lesson even with a good lesson plan or good textbooks. Precisely because of this belief, we all do open lessons and try to improve our teaching skills. If you isolate yourself and do whatever you wish to do, I don't think you can ever conduct good lessons."

Lewis points out that teacher competition in this country is puzzling to the Japanese, as is the practice of singling out individuals for "teacher of the year" awards. In Japan, self-improvement for teachers is rooted in both critical self-reflection and in on-going collaboration. Only by working together do they feel they can improve. "There is much less emphasis on external evaluations (merit reviews, checklist evaluations, etc.) of teachers, and this undoubtedly creates a greater feeling (willingness) of revealing one's weaknesses" (in self-evaluations and collaborations).

I have been fortunate to enjoy opportunities to pursue the scholarship of my craft. Through a connection with Harvard Project Zero, I have been given the keys to a valuable world: a wide community of practicing teachers and educational researchers who want to study together. We meet at Harvard to discuss work and practice.

We visit each other's classrooms. We send each other books. And we talk, endlessly, of what makes for good practice—what works. This group has no name, no organization, and no president. There's not even a list of who is in the group. Membership requires nothing more than a willingness to think carefully about one's teaching.

I was fortunate to be an early part of Outward Bound's effort to expand its scope from exclusively leading wilderness expeditions to include shaping public schools based on its principles. Translating the values of courage, compassion, service, and teamwork from mountain climbing to classroom work is not an easy task. The ten years I've spent working with Expeditionary Learning Outward Bound staff and teachers in its network schools have forced me to analyze my teaching practice and values continually.

We pioneered a professional development model that I think is unusually effective. Based on Outward Bound's model of challenge in the unknown, we invited teachers to be part of a summer learning expedition retreat, a week of intense study and risk-taking. These retreats, called *summits*, are an immersion into a particular theme or topic. I lead summits in geology, architecture, and physiology. During a week of focused activities—cave exploring, mountain climbing, designing buildings, analyzing data, critiquing writing—the group of teachers becomes a team, working together and depending on one another. It is a small version of what an expedition, a thematic journey, could be like with a class of students.

I was honored to work for the past three years as a Carnegie Scholar, meeting with other teachers during the summer and communicating with them all year on researching our own practice and a new vision of scholarship in teaching. This book is a product of that opportunity and support.

The heart of my own scholarship and reflective practice has been my school itself. I'm blessed to be a member of a staff that plans together, gives advice and critique, challenges each other and supports and respects each other, in a school setting that encourages this kind of teamwork. Unlike much of the teaching force of America, I haven't had to pursue my practice in isolation.

A Classroom Story: Inspiration in Teaching

I'm hiking up a steep woodland trail, an old logging road, trudging through autumn leaves, mud, and mist. In my hand is a long shovel. On my back is an old, tan knapsack clunking with crowbars, hammers, garden trowels, and digging claws. Being crushed in the backpack by the metal tools is my lunch and extra water bottles and bags of chocolate chip cookies for my class. At my side is a student we'll call Buddy. He looks over at me: Are you sure you don't want me to carry that pack for you?, he asks again.

Buddy is a big sixth grader. He's rough-hewn and muscular; there's already an adult quality to his jaw, his shoulders, and his neck. He's had a tough life and he's a tough kid—he doesn't smile much. He's been in trouble a lot; over the years Buddy has been a handful for teachers to supervise. Not today. Today he's in his element. He's excited and so am I. He looks over and smiles for no reason.

There's a yell up ahead: Hey, you guys! Look at this! The line of students ahead of me and behind, struggling with shovels and heavy packs, suddenly finds new energy and thrashes ahead to see what's been discovered. Is it crystals? Wait for us!

It's not crystals; we're still quite a ways from the old mine. It's just an outcrop of gray rock. It's a piece of rock anyone would walk by without a glance unless you happened to be one of those odd types who gets excited by rocks. Which I am. My excitement has infected my students.

The rock is a slab of weathered granite, coarsely grained, with a thick vein of milky quartz zagging through it like a lightning bolt. My students have learned to see each rock as a book to be read: a mystery story, a diary of local history written by the earth. They gather around the girls who discovered it. Cool! We discuss how we think it formed, how quickly it cooled and hardened, when the quartz intrusion entered, why there are bands of feldspar in one part; we examine the crystal size and the margins of the intrusion. We stand together in the mist and students reach out and touch the rough wet surface as if it's important to do so, as if the rock holds some kind of forest magic.

Before we reach the mine the mist starts to lift, or maybe we're just getting up above it. The sun starts to filter through the wet leaves above us. The pace picks up as student excitement is bubbling over. How many crystals can we take?! For the hundredth time I give them the same answer: As many as you can carry. They begin to shout to each other through the trees: I think I see it! We're almost there, I can feel it! We're almost there!

We descend a narrow, rocky stretch of trail and suddenly there it is before us: the giant clearing—the old mine. Piles of broken white rock, pits of sandy soil; and sparkling through all of it is the mystical shine of wet-green fluorite crystals. It's like coming to the Land of Oz.

The students cheer. One boy raises his shovel above him and tips back his head like a coyote: Gooooooollllld! he howls. Though there's no gold here his classmates understand him perfectly. They scatter down the hill, throw their backpacks down, and drop to their knees to pick up crystals, stuffing their pockets before they even unpack their tools. Buddy is calm. He looks over at me, drops his pack from his shoulder, shakes his head and smiles.

I drop my gear in the center of the old surface mine and call the class over to demonstrate digging techniques. I show them examples of ground crystals and remind them that the finest fluorite crystal of this color discovered anywhere in the world came from this very spot. It sits today in the Smithsonian. Don't fill your pockets with junk, I warn. Be selective. There's enough here for everyone. Be kind and generous with others. They nod seriously and I release them to search.

Fluorite's crystal shape is cubic. The cubes can be as small as the dice used in games or as large as the foam dice hanging from classic car mirrors. It generally breaks along diagonal cleavage lines which fractures the cubic shape and leaves triangles of crystal or, hopefully, diamond-shaped cleavages that look like the classic gem one sees in a movie—lifted from the dirt and held up to the sun, pointed on the top and bottom. Fluorite comes in a spectrum of colors—dark purple, lavender, blue, pink, cream, yellow, white, green. This site has a distinct color only found in this area of New Hampshire: a striking aqua, the green-blue of a Caribbean bay. Because fluorite is a soft mineral and cleaves easily it is not usually used in jewelry. We gather it today not to include in necklaces but to display in the school and in our homes and to sell in our rock and mineral store.

Most students stake out a small claim and begin digging and sifting through the sandy soil for crystals. As discoveries are made there are shouts and cheers, and students run back and forth to see the size and quality of the latest finds. We dig for hours. Students don't even think to break for water or food; they're in a trance—gold fever. In addition to fluorite the students are uncovering lots of quartz, crystal clusters of clear quartz and yellow citrine clusters. Sometimes the quartz and fluorite are interwoven in the same specimen. The white country rock on which the fluorite sits, a rhyolite, often has beautiful dendritic patterns, dark, fern-like shapes on the white stone. As students show me their discoveries I know we're having a lucky day. I've never seen specimens so good here.

Buddy is working alone. He digs a giant pit with methodical patience and strength. His discoveries are remarkable. I crouch down at the side of his hole and look through his pile of finds. He has large clusters of quartz and fluorite both. He has single fluorite cleavages with fine clarity, as large as strawberries. By the time Buddy leaves this day, his pack holds thirty or forty pounds of stone. Most students in the class can't even lift it. He makes a point of giving good specimens to his classmates who didn't have as much luck. He keeps some great samples but gives out great ones too. Students look up at him with gratitude.

Buddy and I have lunch together on the rocks, in the sun, looking at crystals and discussing them. He holds his favorites up to the light and admires them with me.

Buddy is a challenging student but I have an edge on this challenge. He loves this study and so do I.

On the first day of school the class and I filled four rock tumblers full of rough semi-precious stones. Those tumblers ran day and night in the school boiler room. Once a week for a month we poured the stones out to change the abrasive grit to a smoother mixture and we crowded around the plastic washtub to marvel over the changes. I was as eager as any student to get a close look—we each had our eye on particular stones. On the second day of school we went cave exploring, squeezing through underground rock passageways with flashlights in hand. Buddy couldn't have enjoyed this any more than I did. After that students daily brought in rocks from around their houses or from their trips away; we worked to identify these rocks and "read" their stories. With hardness kits, streak plates, sample specimens, and field guides we took on these mysteries together.

The classroom was arranged like a geology museum. Wooden shelves and dividers were lined with black velvet cloth and covered with mineral displays—fossils, metal ores, rocks from around the world, and crystals of all sizes and colors. My lifetime rock collection and specimens owned by students surrounded us as we worked. They gave an air of importance and care to everything we did. When Buddy entered the room each morning he went right to the displays and picked up rocks, examining them, admiring them. So did I.

One corner of the room was a jewelry center. Students designed and crafted necklaces, rings, key chains, bracelets, and earrings using our polished stones and crystals we'd found or bought wholesale. They worked in the center before school, during school, and after school. When they saw my truck at school on the weekend they tapped on the classroom window to ask to come in to work. I spent time in the jewelry center along with the students making presents for my family and pieces for our class store.

Our study of caves was a perfect companion to our reading the books of Mark Twain. The whole class was gripped by *Tom Sawyer;* one group also read *Huckleberry Finn.* We read and reread the *Tom Sawyer* cave sequences and created original annotated maps of the cave in the story. To do this well, we got professional cave maps and studied them. We had a professional spelunker—an international cave photographer—visit, show slides, and teach us about cave mapping.

We dove deeply into the book *Tom Sawyer.* The whole class walked over to the old town graveyard on a dark morning and reenacted the murder scene over and over with different actors and narrators. Reading wasn't Buddy's favorite activity to be sure, but he understood my love of Mark Twain. The character Huckleberry Finn could have been written for Buddy himself. When Buddy and I conferenced together about his reading questions, essays, and projects he was willing to struggle through the work. Yes, it was hard reading, but it was exciting too.

After our experiences in caves, our work with a spelunker, and our reading of *Tom Sawyer,* each student created an original story that took place underground—a short cave novel. When Buddy wrote his cave novel it wasn't as sophisticated and as long as many others in the class. Writing was a great effort for him. Again I received some inspiration on working with him. We had been underground together; we both remembered the feel, the smell of the wet rock; the strange sense of being inside the earth, the fear, the confusion, the darkness, and the pleasure. In writing conferences I returned him to these sensory memories again and again to make his writing alive and vital. When we had group critiques of novel plots Buddy saw my excitement at the power and cleverness of the other students' ideas. He felt it too. What a thing! To be able to create your own underground mystery story. What an opportunity! There were some amazing plot outlines. Buddy's novel may have been brief and a bit gory but it was powerful; it was a success. When he finished his final draft he was proud and so was I.

We read each other's novels silently and aloud. We copied them and sent them to our professional spelunker expert. We shared summaries of the plots with our Kindergarten buddies and read them excerpts. We put them on display for the community on our cave exhibition night. Some are in my library of powerful models even today.

My colleague Patty Klein, an inspiring teacher, said it simply and well: When you're excited about it, the students get excited about it.

If inspiration and passion are vital to good teaching—and I believe they are—where does that leave us? There are certainly lots of teachers out there with little evident passion. Many teachers seem to be on autopilot, plodding on without showing much life. Students sit in their classes and watch the clock. I certainly had my share of such teachers when I was young; I imagine most people did.

This is something to think about: These teachers didn't start out that way. Most student teachers I work with are full of spirit and passion; they are excited by student achievement and have great visions of their careers ahead. But something happens along the way. What is it that often drains the spirit from teachers the longer they stay in the profession?

It's not hard to figure. The working conditions of the profession are awful. When people ask me why I'm not burned out after twenty-five years in the classroom, I explain that my working conditions are not typical.

I'm trusted in my job. No one stops in at 10:35 to make sure my class is starting a lesson mandated by a rigid school curriculum. When I plan an ambitious project—a fieldwork connection, a classroom presentation by an outside expert—I'm not worried that an administrator or colleague will attack me for deviating from prescribed *time on learning tasks*. As long as my students perform well, in their behavior, character, work, and tests, I'm trusted to make good decisions about time use and curriculum. I'm encouraged to innovate.

I do not teach the exact same material in the same way year after year and I do not teach out of dry textbooks. I design curriculum, continually. I'm always learning, and my excitement in learning is always fresh. Curricular planning isn't capricious or arbitrary at my school; there are of course concepts and facts that need to be covered at my grade level due to state, district, or school priorities. Making sure that I cover world geography or the proper form of a business letter doesn't mean I can't weave these skills into different studies or projects in a different way each year. Even when I teach the same thematic study again (I've taught geology as a theme five times in twenty-five years), I can include new projects that challenge both the class and me.

I have flexibility and control. I design, arrange, and decorate my classroom to realize my vision. I have one group of students whom I see almost all day; I shorten and extend work times as fits the project at hand. I have a classroom budget, allocated on a per-pupil formula, that allows me to spend money as I deem wise: on books, maps, science supplies, art and stationery supplies. Since so much of the curriculum is hand-crafted, I have ready access to photocopying, laminating, and book binding equipment. When our project work entails leaving the building I'm not restricted by rules that limit the number of trips or type of fieldwork allowed.

I have support, *lots* of support. I'm not working alone. I'm part of a community of educators who work together, help and critique each other. We don't agree on everything but we share a vision. We all hand-craft our curriculum; we all love original student work. I'm part of a team of teachers, classroom teachers and special education teachers, who are given the time to plan together and who are supported to work together. The school has adopted structures—exhibitions, assembly presentations, class displays, class partnerships, portfolios—that encourage originality, teamwork, and innovative studies.

I have strong opportunities for professional growth within my school and beyond. Because I have the good fortune to work with education networks and partnerships—Expeditionary Learning Outward Bound, Harvard Project Zero, The Coalition of Essential Schools, The Carnegie Foundation—I am able to examine my own practice, glean ideas from all over, and get an emotional boost from being inspired by other educators and schools. Most teachers hardly have the chance to leave their own building; it's easy to lose touch with the world in other schools.

Many districts do not trust teachers with this kind of responsibility, just as many teachers do not trust their students to build houses or handle delicate scientific equipment in the field. My experience has been that my students have always risen to the job and earned the trust and responsibility offered. It would seem that some schools might do well to consider offering more trust, responsibility, and support to teachers.

To do so requires courage on the part of administrators. In a time when pressure is intense, when principals and teachers are under critical siege and are being evaluated almost entirely on test scores, supporting teacher innovation and spirit is not particularly popular. The push now is to standardize, not innovate.

Inspiration in teaching goes both ways: Good teachers both inspire students and are inspired by students. Teachers in my building are always grabbing my arm in the hallway. Do you have a second?, they ask. Can I show you something really great? And I'm pulled to a bulletin board or into a classroom in which there is a display of student work or the work of a single child to admire. The work of students, the successes of students, the courage and compassion of students—these are what make teaching a fulfilling and gratifying profession. Hardly a day goes by when I don't feel inspired by the effort or kindness of a student in my classroom.

For me, the degree to which students provide inspiration is tied directly to the opportunities I give them. The more I allow students to assume responsibility, the more avenues for creativity or originality I provide them, the greater the chance that their achievements will surprise and inspire me. Powerful, original student writing, clever mathematical ideas, project ideas, beautiful work, transcendent discussion insights—These things inspire me. The student who gives up recesses to help Kindergarten children in their gym class, the student who volunteers to clean up the building grounds, the student who chooses to partner with a challenged child to make sure that child won't feel left out—These things inspire me.

One of the privileges of my teaching environment is that I am permitted and encouraged to let students take on genuine responsibility. In every study I do, students end up redirecting and shaping the course of the investigation or the nature of projects. I am not the type of teacher who can leave things unplanned; I plan all of my studies and assignments compulsively. I am ready, however, to let go of plans when students convince me of the merit of doing so. This negotiation can be as specific as the schedule for the day—a month ago students begged me to change parts of the day's schedule so they could work uninterrupted on their home blueprints. I agreed on two conditions: one, that the time be silent, and two, that they agreed to complete the missed work as homework. They worked intently for two and a half hours straight and felt very pleased that they had won the negotiation. But I didn't feel that I'd lost. Such negotiations can also be as broad as what projects or fieldwork we can accomplish during our study. In many schools I would not have the option of allowing students these opportunities to prove to themselves and to me what they can manage.

A fine example of this is the gem and jewelry store I described earlier. Students were given the responsibility and power to design and manage this store themselves.

I put a lot of planning and commitment into the store: I bought large quantities of rough, semi-precious tumbling stock and tumbling grits; I ordered wholesale batches of jewelry findings—chains, rings, bracelets, key chains, earrings, bell caps, jump rings—to which stones could be attached. I had over eight hundred dollars of my own money sunk into this store and it hadn't even opened; we had nothing yet to sell. But I told the students: This is your store. You will make the decisions, keep the books, design and price the items, and determine store policy. Right now, you're $860 in the red, in debt to me. If you make a profit it will go toward our trip to New York City and to our charity contributions. I trust you'll make good decisions. I wasn't really worried about turning a profit and getting my money back. I knew our enviable position in the market: We would open a few weeks before Christmas as the only store in town.

I taught them to make jewelry and the jewelry-making center opened. Outside experts who made jewelry visited and gave us their professional tips. Students decided the policies for the center: how many could work in the center at once, how the workers would rotate, how many items a worker could make, how stones could be reserved, how quality control would be insured. When we began to run low on supplies I took out the catalogues and students decided what to order and in what quantities. One might think that they would have had trouble exercising restraint in purchases but the truth was many were scared that they'd be in debt to me for the rest of their lives if they bought imprudently, and their orders were thoughtful and wise. They came up with new ideas for items and designs and bought new materials to make these possible. All of this was documented by students in the ledger book.

When the grand opening date grew close we had hundreds of necklaces—silver, gold or black cord with dangling polished stones or quartz crystals or combinations of crystals, stones and beads. We had stud earrings and dangling earrings, stone rings, bracelets and key chains, and a wide assortment of rocks, minerals, and crystals that students had collected on our trips or bought wholesale from suppliers. We had to price each of these. We discussed the approximate unit price of each item, given the cost of materials (our labor was counted as free). Students discussed what degree of mark-up would maximize our profits. Some students wanted to mark up a necklace that cost $1.90 in materials to a price of $10. That's $8.10 in pure profit, they cried. Others thought we should sell them for $2.50: Think of how many more necklaces we'll sell, they argued; in the end we'll profit more. This discussion went on for days and included parent opinions. In the end they were afraid to decide and asked me if I'd set the prices. I refused. It's not my store, I told them.

They settled on a compromise price for all the items. Then a strange thing happened. A student offered a voice of dissent against the hard-fought compromise: I think these prices are too high for our town, she said. I don't think it's fair to people who live here. And so the discussion began again. What was a fair price for the town? Isn't this store partly for profit and partly as a community service for a town that has no stores? Shouldn't we be sensitive to families without much money? What about Kindergartners whose parents won't even let them *bring* money to school?

The students lowered the prices and, in addition, decided to offer discounts to poor families. They decided to make a list of the poor families in town; they went to the school principal to ask for the free lunch list. He wouldn't give it to us, they said sadly when they returned to class. Hey, it doesn't matter, said one student, we know who is poor in town; we can just make our own list. As soon as the list was started students realized how sensitive an issue this was; it was torn up right away.

The eventual pricing policy was not one you'd find at many stores. A clerk working at the jewelry store could offer any discount to a student whenever he or she wanted if the clerk felt the student didn't have enough money. It was to be done sensitively: the clerk was to tell the student confidentially that there was going to be a special sale at recess and to return then. The clerk could then sell anything at any discount without embarrassment to the student. Also, the class instituted a one-cent table on which everything would cost a penny so that little kids could always afford something. If Kindergartners didn't have money, the clerks would slip them some pennies.

When the time came to name the store there was a long list of names considered (The Crystal Corner, Mineral and Gem Shoppe, and such). The names were written on the blackboard and I voted along with the students. When the vote was over I was appalled. That can't be the name, I said. That's awful. They just shook their heads at me. Remember, it's not your store, they said.

Rocks R Us opened on a morning two weeks before the winter holiday. On its first day it grossed almost $1200. Already students were out of the red and collecting profits. They couldn't believe it. They counted the money again and again, danced around with bills in their hands, went over the books together. It was real. Sometimes living in a town with no stores can have its advantages.

In a week we were sold out entirely—not even a penny crystal left. We were proud and exhausted. This can't end, the students said. We need to open a mail-order business, create a brochure, advertise, order new supplies, and get back to the jewelry making!

But I said no. There was too much else to do. I was sorry but after the winter holiday we had to move on.

We did not close up the jewelry-making center. It stayed open all year to handle repairs. The students designed a comprehensive guarantee of their work: If it breaks, we fix it or replace it. No questions asked. When groups of first grade boys came to the classroom with broken necklaces after a rough game at recess they were escorted in politely and my students helped them fill out repair orders.

The repair policy went beyond that of most businesses but my students were proud of it. This is the way the world should be, they said. You should be able to count on quality.

Afterword
Measures of Excellence

I'm standing at a silver airport baggage carousel in Atlanta on a balmy Friday evening in October; another conference. When I drove to school this morning in New England there was frost on my truck and the temperature was in the mid-twenties; it must be in the upper seventies here—it feels a little dreamy. My slides and videotapes are safe in my carry-on bag on my shoulder. My big black portfolio of student work is working its way toward me on the conveyor belt. There's no panic this evening. I've got the student work with me, lots of it. The airport is tense; it's been less than two months since the September 11 tragedy and there is a military presence everywhere. I nod to the soldiers, who look so young, and walk to the shuttle van. I think of my former students who are now in military service; some of them send me regular emails and letters.

There is a fancy Friday-night reception for funders and presenters at the hotel. I change into nicer clothes in my hotel room and arrive at the reception late. There are no familiar faces in the crowd. Several people introduce themselves to me with friendly smiles. When they find out that I'm a classroom teacher in a public school they squint their eyes and nod with admiration, gripping my shoulder and telling me I do *the real work*, the important work. Then they quickly disengage and slip away to meet someone of significance.

I notice that in the corner of the room there are tables holding student work on presentation boards, and there are some actual students standing there beside the work, waiting for questions. I don't know who was responsible for arranging this, but I'm very impressed—what a great idea for this event. I walk over to a line of middle school students, African American boys and girls with serious faces. They are well dressed in a youthful, modern way: the boys with brand new basketball shoes, brand new athletic warm up suits or stiff, large black jeans, the girls with tight pants and glistening braids. I go slowly down the line of tables, asking each about his or her work, and I'm enchanted by their serious explanations and their heartfelt pride. There is something pure in their eyes and their faces that makes me proud to be a teacher. I can't get them to smile at first—they're still nervous—but they speak maturely about their projects. There are black and white photographs of their work at an Atlanta nursing home interviewing senior citizens. The students took these photos themselves and developed and printed them, they explain to me. They show me their biographical writing and when they share stories of the interviews they shake their heads and smile. When I leave and go up to my hotel room I'm already glad I made this trip.

Setting up for the keynote presentation Saturday morning there is a problem. The technical crew laughs at my request for a carousel slide projector instead of a PowerPoint projector. The guys look like they're sixteen years old; they discuss whether they've ever seen a carousel projector being used. We don't even have one of those old projectors, one explains. Luckily the hotel still owns a slide projector so they are able to set it up for me. My presentation goes well. I have some brand new slides of a new study and I'm excited to share them.

I have a morning breakout session after the presentation, a chance to meet with a smaller group of educators for discussion. The group is a mix of teachers and administrators from all over the country; it's diverse racially and diverse in age. The common ground, at the moment, is skepticism. People are enthusiastic about my ideas but they all have the same question: How much of this could possibly work in *my* setting?

I begin the discussion, as always, with a reminder: I have no blueprint to share: this isn't a quick fix. It's an ethic, an approach, a way of thinking. I ask them each to think about the culture of their district, school, or classroom and to reflect on where in that culture they see quality. What do they think contributes to the success in those realms, and what prevents it in other places?

In their own way, almost everyone sees a lack of capacity in their setting. The administrators feel that most of their teachers are not well prepared and lack the potential for high-quality work. Many of the teachers feel the same way about their students. We talk about the need to *build capacity*, rather than seeing it as a fixed resource. This ethic means expecting much more of teachers and students, investing them with much greater responsibility and accountability, and then expecting and supporting them to succeed.

For administrators it means involving school faculties and individual teachers in decision making in genuine and significant ways, including determining school priorities, organization, finances, and hiring. It means trusting and expecting teachers to be professionals in their classrooms with control over and thoughtful judgment concerning curriculum, instruction, and schedules. It means incorporating significant individual and team planning time into a teacher's regular work week and building in school-wide structures that support staff teamwork and sharing. It means building school-wide structures that support the creation and celebration of quality work, such as portfolio systems, exhibitions, presentations, community relationships, grant funding, and even expanded hallway galleries for work. It means modeling an ethic of excellence in maintaining physical facilities and in developing a climate of physical and emotional safety for all students.

It means that administrators should be able to expect from teachers a much deeper and broader level of commitment and accountability—accountability for things that really matter. Rather than teachers feeling that accountability means micro-management —that if the principal walks into their classroom the teacher should be teaching from a particular page of a particular textbook—teachers should feel that accountability means results. This means much more than just test scores. It means that a guest to his or her classroom should find students who are polite, engaged, and articulate about their learning. The room should be filled with attractive displays of high-quality student work—original work, not just commercial worksheets—and good literature or discipline-appropriate reading. Students should be thoughtful and capable in sharing their work (early drafts and final products), and in reflecting on their strengths, their needs, and their goals. The classroom should be impeccable in its climate of personal safety.

It means that teachers should assume a parallel perspective toward their students: higher expectations in everything: more trust, more responsibility, and deeper and broader accountability.

We discuss the strategies, the tools, embedded in the creation of the work I shared. Many of the teachers in the group are already using some of these strategies and using them well, and they share their experiences. Others are intimidated: All of their teaching work is based in textbooks and workbooks, few original assignments. None of the work goes through multiple drafts or gets critiqued or shared with a wider audience.

We discuss the power of thoughtful, original assignments and projects, of real research, of work that allows for critical thinking and discovery. We discuss the power of having an outside audience, of students and teachers making their work public, of the great positive pressure this brings toward improving quality. We discuss using strong and varied models of work to set standards and create a vision of excellence; we talk of the need to build libraries of such models. We discuss the importance of creating rubrics to make clear the requirements of assignments and the attributes that are valued in assignments. And we discuss the ethic of quality as opposed to quantity: building fewer final products but building them really well, working through multiple drafts in a class and school culture of critique.

This is a lot. Many people want to know where to begin. Of course there is no answer to this. Every school is different. There are many entry points. A school or a classroom needs to choose a focus to begin. Start small, I suggest. It is better to improve one aspect of a culture and do it really well than to take on too much too soon and do it poorly. Do something well and build from there. Find something that most people feel good about and willing to tackle, rather than having the idea imposed as a mandate from above.

The discussion ends on a lighter note as people share stories of initiatives in their buildings or districts that were too broad and failed, or stories of change that was forced from outside and made everyone miserable. Everyone has such stories, and here, with a little distance, we can laugh at them.

I've been invited to a working lunch to discuss the next steps for the organization sponsoring the conference. I see many of the faces from the reception last night, though today they show more interest in conversing with me. I get lots of compliments on the student work I shared in the morning but now, I'm told, it's time for the hard questions.

Everything you shared this morning is wonderful, says one gentleman. But it's basically useless unless we can scale it up quickly and scale it up very large. How do you propose scaling this up? Where are you going to find teachers to do this stuff? What kind of training will you have for this teaching system? How many districts can take this on and how quickly?

This all needs to be results driven, data driven, says another gentleman. The work looks good and it's fine but we need baseline data and improvement data for your students, for example, and we need baselines on all these schools we're working with and specific improvement goals and timelines, and we need consequences when they don't meet those results.

Almost all of these men are businessmen; even the members of the educational organization have come from business. I understand and respect their perspectives, and I believe that their impatience stems from a genuine desire to improve schools, particularly urban schools. But in some basic ways, what I do with my life is not business, and business strategies are not always the best model. My daughter started a catering business and she runs it with impeccable standards; it's very successful and I couldn't be more proud of her. When she gets poor quality food deliveries, she sends them back. When I get students with difficulties or poor skills, I can't send them back, nor do I want to. If my daughter's business begins to overtake other caterers and drive them out of business, I'll be pleased for her success. I am not working against other schools and I feel that the children in every school deserve the best—I don't want any school to fail.

The implications of my work seem tenuous or even empty if the only paradigm being discussed is scaling up. Scaling up works for systems, not for an ethic that is built carefully, by hand, over time.

Scaling up is not my goal, I tell the group. Scaling up is taking a restaurant that works and making thousands of them, identical copies, standardized like the fast food restaurants on American highways. This can be useful if you want to make a profit. But I don't want to make a profit; I want to spread ideas. Ideas can proliferate without scaling up and without standardization. When I was a child the diversity of American culture wasn't reflected in restaurants: hot dogs and hamburgers were everywhere but tacos and bagels and sushi were unheard of in most of the country. Now these foods are everywhere. They weren't scaled up; *the idea of including them* just spread everywhere. This is my hope for these ideas, I say. Schools can begin to include them.

Yes, but you need data all the same, says one of the men. What kind of longitudinal data do you have on your students?

I share some data. I don't have a lot, since the interest in longitudinal data is fairly new, but what I have is positive.

As the discussion continues around me, I'm distracted by a deeper question, something beyond the data. How do I really know what I have done for students? How do I know what my school has done for students in the long run? How does one measure something like this?

I think of my life in my small town. The policeman for my town is a former student. I trust him to protect my life; I trust him to work kindly and carefully with the young students in my school, which he does often and does tenderly. The nurse at my medical clinic is my former student. I trust her with my health. The excavator who measured and dug the foundation hole for my house, who built my driveway and septic system, is a former student; I built my home on his work. The lifeguard at the town lake is my former student; she watches my grandsons as they swim. There may not be numbers to measure these things but there is a reason I feel so free and thankful trusting my life to these people: They take pride in doing their best. They have an ethic of excellence.

Acknowledgments

I began documenting my vision and practice under the guidance of Steve Seidel at the Harvard Graduate School of Education in 1989, and I have benefited from his generous wisdom in shaping my writing and thinking ever since. The first iteration of these thoughts was completed under the direction of Steve, Howard Gardner, Dennie Palmer Wolf, Vito Perrone, and a variety of talented educators at Harvard Project Zero. Subsequently, many of these ideas appeared in a publication by the Annenberg Foundation in 1996, *A Culture of Quality*, for which I am indebted to Joe MacDonald as editor and mentor.

Support for this manuscript was made possible through the generosity of the Carnegie Foundation under the leadership of Lee Shulman, through the Carnegie Academy for the Scholarship of Teaching and Learning (CASTLE). CASTLE directors Anne Lieberman and Tom Hatch, teacher Jason Raley, and my fellow Carnegie Scholars provided direction and critique for me in three summer institutes that catalyzed and clarified my work.

The Expeditionary Learning Outward Bound school network, under the leadership of Greg Farrell and Meg Campbell, has been a center for my professional growth for the past decade. I have had the privilege to work with a number of gifted educators through my affiliation with Expeditionary Learning. In particular, Scott Hartl, Kathy Greeley, and Steven Levy have had an ongoing and profound influence on my thinking and practice for ten years and continue to do so as colleagues, mentors, and friends.

My teaching practice is most deeply indebted to the staff of the Shutesbury Elementary School who have inspired my growth for twenty-five years. The foundation of my practice I credit to Ken Lindsay, Patty Klein, David Potter, Heather Lobenstine, Judy Nerbonne, Susan Fletcher, Bonnie Roy, Bob Dihlmann, Katie Bloomfield, Bernice Carew, Terri Wells, Vicki Davey, Karen Anolik, Laura Baker, Les Edinson, Tom Jefferson, Barbara Fisher, and Pat Guild. In addition to my Shutesbury colleagues, I am indebted to Hampshire College professors John Reid and Merle Bruno, and to Eileen Mariani and Bill Simmons, former teaching partners.

I was fortunate to have the expert guidance of Kate Montgomery, my editor at Heinemann, in shaping the manuscript for publication.

Lastly, I am grateful for the ubiquitous support of my wife, Elaine, who understands my impassioned educational pursuits.